Under the supervision of
FRANÇOIS COLCOMBET

Where is Iran heading?

Regime's battle for supremacy or survival?

Paris, France
May 2017

Publication of Foundation for Middle Eastern Studies
(La Fondation d'Etudes pour le Moyen-Orient)
www.fondationfemo.com

CONTENT

PREFACE

Frédéric Encel

At present, many observers tend to interpret Iranian political or military initiatives in the Middle East as demonstrations of its strength, whereas they should above all be seen as signs of internal weakness. In reality, the mullahs' regime is facing considerable opposition from the people.

The Iranian nuclear agreement, concluded on July 14, 2015 in Vienna between Iran and the P5+1 group (the five permanent members of the Security Council and Germany) and UN Security Council Resolution 2231, which ratifies the agreement, raised hopes about a possible normalization of relations with this great nation, as well as a calming of the situation in the Middle East. In addition, a number of nations were counting on this opening-up to invest and/or locate their productions in this great country.

The arrival in Washington of Donald Trump – who had sworn he would shred the Iranian nuclear deal – dampened the enthusiasm, even though it seemed that the new American administration would renegotiate the terms rather than just tear up the agreement altogether. At least, Trump still says he wants to monitor the strict application of the clauses of the agreement, with no complacency.

But apart from this affair, what would considerably embarrass the Iranian regime is the adoption of new sanctions against Iranian companies and institutions involved in terrorism, human rights violations or the Iranian Revolutionary Guards' ballistic missiles program. The majority of Iranians are not feeling any beneficial effects whatsoever from the first relaxations of sanctions having occurred since January 2016; but the regime remembers the major uprising of 2009 and fears a rise in exasperation that could overturn it.

From a social and economic viewpoint, a recent IMF report rightly states that the Iranian economy is threatened by "renewed uncertainty" because of the possibility of new sanctions against Tehran hampering the business environment. "The current account position has remained in surplus, despite the sharp drop in oil prices, due to the rapid rebound in oil exports, and strengthening non-oil exports (e.g., automobiles and petrochemicals) following the lifting of sanctions," is notably what the International Monetary Fund wrote in its annual report on the Iranian economy. According to its estimates, Iran's Gross Domestic Product grew by 6.5% in 2016, after having contracted by 1.6% the previous year. It adds that "The renewed uncertainty surrounding the JCPOA, and especially relations with the U.S., could deter investment and trade with Iran and short-circuit the anticipated recovery." US sanctions and related uncertainty have hindered the return of global banks to the Iranian market.

Now, after some ballistic missile tests, the US administration has imposed new sanctions linked to that program and has accused Tehran of being the biggest state sponsor of "terrorism" on the planet, and the Islamic Revolutionary Guards Corps (the *Pasdaran*) are likely to be placed on the list of terrorist organizations. For a country of which more than 50% of the economy is dominated by the Pasdaran, such a situation would have serious consequences.

Lastly, with regard to human rights, President Rouhani's "moderate" government has not scored any points, and Iran continues to hold the record for executions per capita. Opponents, intellectuals, artists, sexual minorities (homosexuals) and religious minorities (Baha'i faith) continue to be persecuted by an authoritarian religious regime, with practices sometimes reminiscent of those of the Middle Ages.

One factor complicates the situation yet more: the regional policy of the Iranian regime – which is imbued with a faint tendency towards imperialism with, as the alibi, a type of pan-Shiism that can be seen in Iraq, Syria, Lebanon and Yemen. Sometimes, the attitudes of the Shiite militias supported by Tehran are evocative of Daesh in their cruelty. This is why the Iranian regime is increasingly being blamed by nations in the region as being a source of trouble, problems and instability rather than solutions. So, once the wind of enthusiasm from the West has faded out, it may be a long time until it swings again behind the Iranian theocracy. On the other hand, the genuine interest in the great civilization that Iran is, plus the intellectual richness of its people and its high level of engineering, could persuade the world to go along with it in its quest for emancipation and its defiance vis-à-vis obscurantism.

From this viewpoint, the recent death of former President Ali-Akbar Hashemi Rafsanjani – one of the principal pillars of the regime since its beginning but also, especially, the cornerstone of the so-called "pragmatic" current – durably darkens the chances of a far-reaching internal reform of the system. Henceforth, the Supreme Leader will doubtlessly feel less restrained in his will to uniformize the regime. We are reminded that, during a past attempt to achieve dominance and take full control over the reins of power, to the detriment of the opposing clan during the presidential elections of 2009, it contributed to igniting a genuine Iranian Spring (two years before the Arab Spring), with the associated peaceful demonstrations and repression.

Today, having lost its internal balance, the Iranian regime fears that it is moving toward a troubled period that may lead to the Islamic Republic's downfall. This work strives to shed some light on the Iranian enigma and its regional consequences.

Frédéric Encel is a geopolitique researcher and a professor of international relations at Paris School of Business.

A failed bet: The nuclear deal and Iran's strategic behavior

Bruno Tertrais

The bet made by the Obama administration has failed.

From Washington's point of view, a deal with Tehran on the nuclear issue was to be a path towards a new strategic relationship with Iran, a tool to moderate the country's behavior and a way to reintegrate it in the world community. It was a de facto "grand bargain".

This has not happened. The nature of the Islamic Republic has not changed. Its nuclear program remains fraught with uncertainties. Its missile program continues unabated. Its support for terrorism and destabilizing role in the region is intact.

There have been additional costs. The bet explains largely for instance why the Obama administration refrained from significantly helping the Syrian opposition or intervening massively in the country – a decision which indirectly contributed to shoring up the Damascus regime.

Overall, what was the centerpiece of the US policy in the region appears, almost two years later, as a real failure.

Internal Dynamics

The July 2015 nuclear deal has not changed the domestic politics of Islamic Republic.

In May 2016, the Assembly of Experts chose hardliner ayatollah Ahmad Jannati as its chairman. A week later, leading conservative MP Ali Larijani was reelected speaker of the Majlis. At the same time, two state-sponsored cultural organizations held an exhibition of the "best" Holocaust cartoons in Tehran, a contest that had been announced in December 2015. An anti-Semitic French cartoonist was the winner.

In a major speech given on the occasion of the 27th anniversary of the death of his predecessor ayatollah Khomeini, Supreme Leader Ali Khamenei stated that trusting or cooperating with the United States would be a mistake, since "the US will never stop its destructive role". He qualified the United States, but also Britain and Israel, as "enemies".[1]

The September 2016 report of the United Nations Secretary General on the "Situation of human rights in the Islamic Republic of Iran" was damning. It stated:

"Human rights violations have continued at an alarming rate. In particular, a significant number of executions took place, including of individuals who were juveniles at the time of the alleged offence; corporal punishment, including flogging, persisted; the treatment of journalists and human rights defenders remained of concern, as raised by several United Nations human rights mechanisms; and religious and ethnic minorities continued to face persecution and prosecution."[2]

In 2015, 966 persons were executed, the highest number in over

---

[1] Rick Gladstone, « Iran's Supreme Leader on America : Don't Trust, Don't Cooperate », The New York Times, 3 June 2016.

[2] Situation of human rights in the Islamic Republic of Iran, Report of the Secretary General, A/71/374, United Nations, 71st session, 6 september 2016.

two decades, in continuation of an upward trend for more than ten years. The Islamic Republic ranks number one in the world in terms of executions per capita and of executions of children.

On February 10, 2017, as has been the case every year since 1980, thousands rallied in Tehran chanting "Death to America!", "Death to Israel!", while some burnt US and Israeli flags.[3] That same day, ayatollah Khamenei made it clear that he felt vindicated in his view of the United States, given that president Trump "largely did the job for us in revealing true face of America" (sic).[4] In a speech given in late February, Khamenei used inflammatory language about Israel and recalled the goal of a "complete liberation of Palestine".[5]

To all those studying the behavior of the Iranian regime, this attitude was not a surprise. Ayatollah Khamenei wanted to show that he remained in charge and that the fundamentals of the revolution would not be questioned. He could not, and cannot afford the more pragmatic elements of the regime, such as president Rowhani, to gain power and prestige.

The Nuclear Program

Obama's number one foreign policy priority has even largely failed in its immediate purpose: it has not produced a credible, long-term solution to the nuclear problem.

To be clear, epithets such as "Munich" are unwarranted. The nuclear deal – the Joint Comprehensive Plan of Action (JCPOA) - was certainly not the triumph heralded by the Obama administration, but it slowed the Iranian program and has made it

---

[3] « 'Death to America' : Thousands rally in Iran celebrating Islamic Revolution », Associated Press, 10 February 2017.

[4] @khamenei_ir, 2:36 PM - 7 February 2017.

[5] Reuters, « Iran's Khamenei Call On Palestinians to Continue Intifada Against Israel », 21 February 2017.

less tempting, at least for a while, to "break out". The required time to produced one Significant Quantity (SQ) of highly enriched uranium was lengthened from 2-3 months to about a year.

However, at the same time, the deal's flaws are numerous.

-   It has given the Islamic Republic a free pass on its previously detected military activities. The investigation into such activities was closed in December 2015 – a "premature" decision according to the best experts.[6]
-   It did not require Iranian adhesion to the conventions on civilian nuclear security.
-   It has decreased the level of transparency requested to Iran. The UNSC resolutions demanding specific access to certain sites, activities or individuals were superseded. Publicly, we now know less about the Iranian program than was the case before the deal: IAEA reports are now about a third the length of what they used to be.[7]

While Iran has not been formally accused of violations of the deal as of this writing (March 2017), there have been several troubling developments:

-   While barely using the dedicated procurement channel set up by the deal, Iran is suspected to have illicitly acquired materials for its program such as carbon fiber.[8]
-   Tehran has announced it would develop nuclear-powered vessels; this raises question since reactors powered with low-enriched uranium would be a very costly achievement,

---

[6] Olli Heinonen, Ensuring Iran's Enrichment R&D is for Peaceful Purposes, Foundation for the Defense of Democracies Policy Brief, 26 January 2017, p.1.

[7] Valerie Lincy & Gary Milholin, Iran's Nuclear Veil, Iran Watch, 1 February 2017.

[8] Ryan Browne, « German intelligence: Iran may have tried to violate nuclear deal », CNN.com, 8 July 2016.

while higher percentage enriched uranium is forbidden by the deal.[9]
- Iran has produced heavy water in excess of the JCPOA's provisions.[10]
- Through imports, Tehran is stockpiling natural uranium in quantities that are not required by its current and foreseeable needs.[11]

- In 2016, Tehran started introducing enriched uranium in modern, efficient IR-6 centrifuges.[12] In 2017, it announced that it would start testing the newest IR-8 models.[13] If Iran built a sufficiently high number of IR-8, its breakout time would be dramatically reduced.

Some claim that nuclear cooperation between Iran and North Korea is real and continuing.[14]

Reports of the International Atomic Energy Agency since the entry into force of the deal include fewer details than in the past. Notably, they do not say whether Iran is fully compliant with the deal, whether suspect sites have been visited, nor whether the Agency is in a position to verify the absence of undeclared nuclear

---

[9] Reuters, « Iran to work on nuclear-powered vessels after US 'violation' of deal », 13 December 2016.

[10] David Albright and Andrea Stricker, Analysis of the IAEA's Fourth Iran Deal Report : Time of Change, Institute for science and international security, 15 November 2016.

[11] Olli Heinonen, Iran Stockpiling Uranium Far Above Current Needs, Foundation for the Defense of Democracies Policy Brief, 10 January 2017.

[12] David Albright and Andrea Stricker, Analysis of the IAEA's Fourth Iran Deal Report : Time of Change, Institute for science and international security, 15 November 2016.

[13] Olli Heinonen, Ensuring Iran's Enrichment R&D is for Peaceful Purposes, Foundation for the Defense of Democracies Policy Brief, 26 January 2017.

[14] Refael Ofek & Dany Osham, Iran Is Progressing Towards Nuclear Weapons Via North Korea, BESA Center Perspectives Paper, n° 415, 28 February 2017.

material in the country. To use the words of respected experts, it is likely that Tehran – as predicted by many analysts – is "pushing the envelope of compliance".[15]

One should also note that from a more general non-proliferation standpoint, the deal is problematic since it has not only wiped Iran's state clean on weaponization activities but also, for the first time, legitimized a uranium enrichment program that never had a clear civilian rationale.

Tehran's Missiles

Tehran's missile program has continued unabated since the Vienna 2015 agreement. Between July 2015 and February 2017, it may has tested as many as fourteen ballistic missiles.[16]

Twice in the fall of 2015, Iran violated UNSC Resolution 1929 (2010) when it tested medium-range ballistic missiles.

Since the JCPOA "Implementation Day" on January 16, 2016, the new operative UNSC Resolution 2231 has this to say about missiles:

"Iran is called upon not to undertake any activity related to ballistic missiles designed to be capable of delivering nuclear weapons, including launches using such ballistic missile technology, until the date eight years after the JCPOA Adoption Day or until the date on which the IAEA submits a report confirming the Broader Conclusion, whichever is earlier".[17]

The problem with this language is that it is less restrictive than

---

[15] David Albright and Andrea Stricker, Analysis of the IAEA's Fourth Iran Deal Report : Time of Change, Institute for science and international security, 15 November 2016, p. 1.

[16] Behnam Ben Taleblu, Iranian Ballistic Missile Tests Since The Nuclear Deal, Foundation for the Defense of Democracies Research Memo, 9 February 2017.

[17] UNSCR 2231 (2015), Annex B, paragraph 3.

the prior prohibition on missile testing contained in UNSC Resolution 1929 (2010), which said that Iran "shall not undertake any activity related to ballistic missiles capable of delivering nuclear weapons." This restriction was replaced by UNSC Resolution 2231. Furthermore, UNSCR 2231 is ambiguous on what would constitute a violation.

Tehran has continued to test-launch ballistic missiles after Implementation Day. Unreported on national television – perhaps to probe US reactions – Iran's launch of a medium-range missile in January 2017 has not been considered a violation of that resolution by the UN Security Council. Such tests are however, at the very least, inconsistent with the spirit of UNSCR 2231, as described by the UN Secretary General's Reports.

Iran may also have tested a nuclear-capable long-range cruise missile. Such missiles are not covered by UNSCR 2231.[18]

In September 2016, Defense Minister Hossein Dehghan declared that Iran would soon start the production of Khorramshahr and Sejjil long-range missiles.[19] In February 2017, Deputy Commander of the IRGC General Hossein Salami stated that "Each day, the number of [Iran's] missiles, warships and defensive missile launchers will be increased".[20]

Lest one thinks that such programs are mostly conducted for "prestige" reasons, a number of recent statements have reiterated what their targets could be. A senior member of the Majlis and former advisor to the Iranian Supreme Leader's Representative at the IRGC declared in 2017 that "if the enemy makes a mistake", the

---

[18] Reuters, « Iran tested nuclear-capable cruise missile : German newspaper », 2 February 2017.

[19] Farzin Nadimi, « Iran's Latest Missile Test : Scenarios and Implications for the new Administration », The Washington Institute, 3 February 2017.

[20] Rohollah Faghihi, « Iran brushes off being 'put on notice' », Al Monitor, 2 February 2017.

US Fifth Fleet headquarters in Bahrain would be "razed to the ground"; and in addition that, should a missile be fired at Iran, "only seven minutes" would be needed for an Iranian missile "to hit Tel Aviv".[21]

Iranian Aggressiveness and Support for Terrorism

Tehran's actions in its neighborhood can be described as a mix of imperial Persia, revolutionary Iran, and to some extent Shi'a messianism.

The IRI does not really have a grand strategy. It is a mostly opportunistic power. But it has a vision, an ability to think and invest in the long-term. It is very good at being opportunistic, at taking advantage of civil unrest and power vacuums, as for instance it did in Lebanon, Gaza, Iraq or Yemen. It also has an uncanny ability to "fuse" the power of State and non-State actors (Shi' militias but also groups such as Hamas and the Palestinian Islamic Jihad, and today some Taliban groups) to gain regional influence and check its opponents (the United States, Israel and Saudi Arabia mainly).

One effect of the nuclear deal is that Iran's actions in the region are less constrained by financial resources than there were in the past.

Iran has some indirect responsibility in the rise of the Islamic State: it supported the sectarian policies of the Nuri al-Maliki government and contributed to the feeling of disenfranchisement of many Sunnis.

Recently, it has empowered the Badr Organization to operate autonomously from Hezbollah, and on a par with it, reporting

---

[21] « Senior MP: Iran to Demolish US Base in Bahrain in Case of Aggression », Fars News, 5 February 2017.

directly to the IRGC.[22] Even though Shia militias are de facto allies of the United States in the fight against the Islamic State in Iraq, such forces continue to hold very negative views of Washington. The spokesperson of a key Iranian-backed group in the battle for Mosul, Kitaeb Hezbollah, recently declared: "We look at America as our first enemy, the source of all evil on Earth".[23]

The prospect of a deal was one key reason behind the US decision to avoid any significant intervention in the Syrian civil war.

Iranian involvement in the country has been massive since the summer of 2015 – at the same time the nuclear deal was being finalized – when Tehran answered positively to the regime's call for increased support in light of the desperate situation of its armed forces at the time. The Iranian "surge" began in earnest around the same time as Moscow's intervention began in September 2015. Teheran has involved and rotated thousands of troops from the Artesh (its regular armed forces), the IRGC (the Qods force in particular) and the Basij Organization (militias). They played a key role in the recapture of Aleppo.

The Iranian experience in Syria has allowed the country to make a quantum leap in its ability to conduct complex and long-term military operations far from its borders. Simply put, Iran has mutated from a country mostly relying on "asymmetric" and "hybrid"-type operations to a true regional military power, something it had not been since the Iran-Iraq war. What makes this development truly remarkable is that Tehran has simultaneously maintained and improved its ability to operate alongside and in coordination with Shi'i militias in Syria (Hezbollah) and in Iraq. Iranian forces have also largely learned from their Russian

---

[22] Hanin Ghaddar, « Iran May Be Using Iraq and Syria as a Bridge to Lebanon », The Washington Institute, 23 November 2016.

[23] Liz Sly & Loveday Morris, « Trump wants to push back against Iran, but Iran is now more powerful than ever », The Washington Post, 5 February 2017.

counterparts, notably for special operations, air assault operations, and joint (air/land) operations.[24]

Iran is now firmly entrenched in Syria and is there for the long haul. It has finally built and consolidated a real "strategic bridge" to the Mediterranean. According to a recent in-depth analysis of the Iranian military campaign in Syria,

"Iran ultimately seeks to ensure that Iranian proxies can use Syrian territory as a vehicle to project influence into the Levant and maintain a deterrence infrastructure against Israel. (..) The Iranian regime recognizes its proxies in Syria as part of its Axis of Resistance coalition on which Iran can rely to contain the U.S. and its regional allies. An opportunity for Iran to consolidate its influence in Syria translates into an expanded capability to use Syrian territory as a staging point to conduct operations throughout the region to the ultimate detriment of U.S. interests and allies in the Middle East."[25]

In Syria, the West and the IRI continue to have fundamentally different interests. Iran seeks primarily to save its only real ally – the Damascus regime – maintain its connection with Hezbollah, and ensure access to the Mediterranean. The fight against ISIS is a relatively minor goal of Tehran in Syria.

On the 38th anniversary of the revolution, IRGC leaders boasted that its ideology has now reached the Mediterranean Sea and beyond.[26]

The nuclear deal has not changed Iranian support for terror. Tehran is still the world's leading sponsor according to the United

---

[24] « Téhéran et l'école russe », TTU, n° 1051, 8 February 2017.

[25] Paul Bucala, Iran's New Way of War in Syria », Institute for the Study of War, February 2017, p. 11, p. 13.

[26] « Iranian official : our revolution has gone beyond the Mediterranean », Al-Arabiya, 11 February 2017.

States government.[27] As confirmed by its leader Hassan Nasrallah, "Hezbollah's budget, its income, its expenses, everything it eats and drinks, its weapons and rockets, are from the Islamic Republic of Iran".[28] Support for Hamas has also been reconfirmed, notably at the occasion of a high-profile conference held in Tehran in February 2017.[29]

Other actions since the summer of 2015 show that Tehran remains a destabilizing force in the region. In 2016, Iran detained ten US soldiers believed to have accidentally wandered into its waters; also, during that year, Iranian speedboats harassed US ships at several occasions.[30] In 2017, Iranian-backed Houthi rebels attacked a Saudi warship shouting "Death to America! Death to Israel! Curse be upon the Jews!" a classic Islamic Republic set of slogans.[31] It would certainly be a stretch to describe Houthis in Yemen as "Iranian stooges". But the Islamic Republic has been supporting them for a decade as proxies against Saudi Arabia, albeit in a limited way. Since the summer of 2014 and the takeover of Sana'a, Tehran has stepped up such support through weapons transfers and assistance for training. While it has not brought about any significant change in the dynamics of the conflict, it represents an investment for the future.[32] Finally, there are

---

[27] Agence France-Presse, « Iran 'biggest state sponsor of terrorism' : Mattis », 4 February 2017.

[28] Agence France-Presse, « Hezbollah brushes off US sanctions, says money comes via Iran », 24 June 2016.

[29] Ali Hashem, « Why Iran wants Palestine back on the regional agenda », Al Monitor, 24 February 2017.

[30] Thomas Erdbrink, « Iran, Puzzled by Trump, Treads Carefully for Now », The New York Times, 2 February 2017.

[31] The video was available on https://twitter.com/spectatorindex/status/826225586309734402

[32] Thomas Juneau, « Iran's policy towards the Houthis in Yemen : a limited return on a modest investment », International Affairs, vol. 92, n° 3, 16 May 2016.

indications that Iranian-supported terrorist cells in Bahrain have grown and expanded.[33]

Conclusion

The judgment of history is still open on the final outcome of the nuclear deal as a non-proliferation instrument. It is already clear, however, that it did not have the slightest positive effect on the general behavior of the Islamic Republic of Iran.

The good news is that the IRI is not as powerful and influential as it would like to believe. Its influence in Iraq was probably stronger a decade ago: the current government resents its meddling in Iraqi affairs. Its involvement in Syria has created resentment in the Arab world. Some in the Hezbollah resent being used as tools of Iranian designs. And from an economic standpoint, Iran remains vulnerable. Structurally low oil prices limit State revenues, and the indirect economic bonanza from the deal is not as important as Tehran expected.

Bruno Tertrais is Deputy Director of the French Fondation pour la recherche stratégique and expert on géopolitiques

---

[33] Matthew Levitt and Michael Knights, Iranian-Backed Terrorism in Bahrain : Finding a Sustainable Solution, Policy Watch 2750, The Washington Institute, 11 January 2017.

With the World Lacking a Common View of Iran, Tehran Takes Advantage

Lincoln P. Bloomfield Jr.

Compared to most governments, Iran's clerical leaders have defied convention. While countries normally strive to be better known and understood in order that their national interests may be respected by others, Iran's ruling regime thrives on quite the opposite phenomenon: being misunderstood. Put differently, the actions, motives and goals of the fundamentalists in Tehran are not openly debated and clearly articulated, and most outsiders who call themselves experts look for and find whatever statements or bits of evidence reinforce their own respective views. The result is that the revolutionary government that has held power in Iran for the past 38 years is perceived differently by at least seven different major constituencies within and outside the country.

In the United States, uncertainty about the true nature of Iran's leadership philosophy and the resulting disagreement over whether engagement with, or resistance to, Iran offers the more prudent course has benefited the clerics, who undoubtedly welcome divisive policy debates about Iran policy in Washington. While Tehran surely anticipated that the 2015 nuclear agreement with the P5+1 governments, although supported by the UN and by many arms control experts in Washington, would face harsh criticism as well in the US, Iranian officials correctly saw many advantages that justified the effort.

Not only was a possible military strike against nuclear sites in Iran averted, but the agreement gained Tehran access to major financial assets, the legitimacy of being courted respectfully by the world's major powers for almost two years, the lifting of the arms embargo, western silence and inaction throughout the talks about Iran's domestic repression and regional destabilization, and the granting of legal status to Iran's nuclear activities in the future – including becoming a nuclear weapons state after the agreed restraints expire.

Notwithstanding the sanctions regime in place prior to the nuclear accord, forceful and unified international condemnation of specific violations of universal rights and norms by Iran has not been seen in recent years. Years of clandestine regime support for credentialed experts in western countries disputing criticism of Iran, defaming the regime's exiled resistance and any who stand with them, cautioning against confrontation and urging instead a path of engagement suggests that a concerted international focus on the government's serial transgressions against its own citizens and neighboring populations would be challenging for the mullahs to manage.

By acknowledging these troublesome issues only in broad rhetorical terms as a longstanding irritant that has already been politically addressed by sanctions, most of the world's governments have shown little interest in the question of why the Iranian regime engages in such behavior. Far more analysis by American foreign policy experts can be found regarding the nature of Russian, Chinese or North Korean politics than the politics of revolutionary Iran. Absent such interest, western governments appear uninterested in the rather central question of whether Iran's leadership is secure in its power and carrying out its intended destiny, or acting out of vulnerability to long-suppressed popular disaffection, seeking to forestall an unstoppable Persian Spring.

As the regime's second Supreme Leader, Ali Khamenei, faces advanced age and reported medical issues, Iran is drawing toward a significant inflection point, a time when its ruling circle, left to their own devices, will attempt to rejuvenate the fortunes of the modern world's first sovereign state purporting to be a religious domain. If the world is looking to discourage the permanent imposition of Islamic caliphates rivaling the Westphalian system of state-based political organizations by which 21st century societies have agreed to live, what happens next in Iran is of no small consequence. That is why the clerics in Tehran fear nothing more than a unified international response to their many provocations.

To explore these differences in perception about Iran, we consider here the perspectives and interests of several different constituencies.

Iran's Clients: Shi'ite Militias and Mercenaries, Sunni Terrorists

It may appear obvious to list entities and individuals directly on the payroll of the Iranian regime such as Lebanon's Hizballah, whose leader has openly acknowledged that the organization is entirely funded by Iran. Yet the size and scope of non-Iranian paramilitary groups, militias and individual fighters is significant, and imposes annual costs likely measured in the tens of billions of dollars that are being diverted from alternative uses benefiting the lives of Iran's 79 million citizens.

With Tehran carrying such a financial burden even in a situation where no significant western effort has been mobilized to pressure the Syrian government, Iranian forces and their proxies as well as Russia to desist from their assaults on populated Syrian cities and towns, two questions arise: first, is this simply a costly exercise in the service of the Iranian revolution, or is the heavy cost borne by Iran, in lives of its soldiers as well as money, evidence of a defensive campaign, signaling that Tehran fears the consequences to its own power of a political transition in Damascus? And second, would the application of meaningful military pressure against the Iran-led presence in Syria, in support of the UN-backed political transition process, expose a deep vulnerability of the Iranian regime, already facing pressures to address domestic economic hardships?

From regime media outlets the answer has been given: the clerics regard Bashar al Assad's regime in Damascus as a vital firewall against the eastward spread of popular protest and potential regime collapse as was experienced in Tunisia and Egypt in 2011. The author's own conversation with Bashar al Assad during a visit of analysts to Syria in January 2009 made clear that the alliance between a secular Alawite dictatorship and the fundamentalists of Iran was purely a marriage of convenience. Iran's financial support to Sunni Islamic extremists including Hamas and Palestinian Islamic Jihad, at a time when Iranian forces and Shi'a proxy militias and fighters have waged sectarian warfare against predominantly Sunni communities in Iraq and Syria, indicates a tactical focus in Tehran that is devoid of religious design or principle.

Iran's Allies and Potential Friends: Russia and China

Throughout the nuclear negotiations beginning in the fall of 2013, one heard diplomats representing the US and its European allies UK, France and Germany repeatedly speak as though the P5+1 countries – the aforementioned four plus Russia and China – were united in their thinking regarding the potential bargain to be struck with Iran. These governments maintained the appearance of a shared strategic perspective throughout the process, culminating in agreement of the parties to the Joint Comprehensive Plan of Action (JCPOA) on July 14, 2015.

In the final days – literally the final hours – of the nuclear talks, a non-nuclear issue was added to the package, and the US consented to the lifting of the international conventional arms embargo on Iran. This concession was granted even though no reciprocal restrictions were required, or pledges solicited, by the P5+1 relating to Iran's use of military weapons against neighboring Iraq and Syria despite more than three years of Iranian paramilitary aggression in both countries, and the takeover of the Hadi government in Sana'a, Yemen by the Iran-supplied Houthi fighters just five months previously.

Perhaps Russia had diligently adhered to the arms embargo, in spirit as well as letter, prior to the lifting of the embargo. But within very short order, agreement was announced for the sale of the S-300 long-range surface-to-air missile system to Iran by Russia; deliveries were made within one year. While this arms transfer may have been planned prior to the arms embargo, the growth of trade in both sensitive military items as well as industrial and manufactured exports from Russia to Iran suggests that the two countries had shared an agenda for expanded relations even as Russian diplomats sat with Iran's counterparties in the nuclear talks.

It is clear that, separately from the nuclear talks, Russia shared common cause with Iran in defending the embattled Assad regime in Damascus. Barely a year after the nuclear agreement was reached, Russia's defense ministry announced that its Tu-22 bombers had staged bombing attacks against targets in Syria flying out of an Iranian base near Hamadan in western Iran. Stationing of military forces on another country's sovereign territory with the host country's full consent, and waging combat operations from there, is a strong measure that two countries are engaged in a de facto alliance.

While China has not made the kind of overt diplomatic or military moves with Iran that Russia has done, there is a history of major Chinese arms sales to Iran during the 1980s and the early 1990s before international sanctions curbed this relationship. Today, China has a considerably more advanced arms industry than it did twenty years ago, and ambitions to support its defense industrial sector through arms sales. China's ability to deliver major weapons systems at substantially lower prices than comparable US or European systems (which of course are not being offered to Iran) will likely appeal to Iran given popular pressures inside Iran for economic relief.

Where China finds political alignment with Iran is the fact that both countries are one-party dictatorships with no provision for ever yielding power. While the same might be said about Russia under Vladimir Putin, China shares a further common cause with Iran insofar as the Chinese government has for decades championed the international norm of "non-interference in the internal affairs" of a state. As the world focuses on the extremely high per capita rate of executions in Iran and the heavily-controlled, undemocratic nature of its Presidential elections in particular, the clerical leaders in Tehran undoubtedly appreciate China's position that these matters – and the frequent evidence of internal popular disaffection – are not legitimate subjects of concern for the international community.

Europe

There is risk of inaccuracy, unfairness and offense in an American observer seeking to characterize European attitudes and positions regarding Iran. In hopes of minimizing that risk, the observation here starts with a self-awareness that the United States sometimes becomes intractable in its moralistic approaches to the world, such that it is not clear what standard the Americans are observing in their efforts to reduce conflict and tensions among states. Europe has its own views of Iran and the Middle East region, informed by a much longer and deeper history of involvement with the peoples and problems involved in today's circumstances than that of the Americans.

And yet, it is the Americans who are expected to set the tone and the course for western relations with Iran – whether insisting on punitive sanctions, or seeking rapprochement as President Obama did beginning in 2013 in announcing the start of nuclear negotiations. The US spends so much more on defense of the transatlantic alliance than any other ally, and has been the superpower partner of choice for most Arab countries as well as Israel for over 35 years, creating an expectation in Europe that on important issues of alliance solidarity such as how to deal with a threatening Iran, some deference will be shown to American policy.

Nevertheless, European foreign policy, while in some ways more moralistic than American, has traditionally been far less inclined to restrict commerce as a tool of foreign policy. Iran under the mullahs has had considerable trade relations with European countries even when foreign and defense ministries were concerning themselves with Iranian terrorism and other serious misbehavior. Moreover, while Europe has been victimized by the clerical regime of Tehran, it is the US whose Embassy was sacked and occupied by Ayatollah Khomeini's followers, and pro-regime crowds have chanted "Death to America" – not "Death to Europe" – for nearly four decades.

There is no doubt that the UK, France and Germany, as members of the P5+1 group negotiating nuclear restraints with Iran, were as concerned as the US that the terms of the JCPOA effectively block any Iranian pathways to the bomb. Indeed, it is well known that during a key juncture in the talks, the French government took a stronger line and persuaded the US side to harden its position out of concern that too much latitude was being given to the Iranian side.

However, in the aftermath of the agreement, it is no less striking that Europe has taken a markedly different approach than the US in authorizing, indeed promoting, major commercial deals with Iran now that sanctions have been lifted. On the US side, the Obama Administration actively encouraged American companies to do business with Iran, recognizing that engaging with the Iranian people would likely yield longer-term benefits by lessening hostility between the two and thus giving more latitude to their governments to explore a less hostile relationship.

The complication for American companies has been that US law continues to ban commercial engagement with entities tied to the regime; and while there is no clear guide to Iran's "front companies," sanctions experts continue to warn American companies that they face likely prosecution in dealing with all but a fraction of Iranian commercial entities, such is the extent of regime control over the country's private sector. While the American airplane manufacturer Boeing has been pursuing a major sale of commercial aircraft to Iran, this potential transaction has been politically controversial and faces significant opposition in the US Congress.

Europe, by contrast, has not seemed to labor under such constraints, whether imposed by law or policy. The day after the nuclear accord was reached, the French Foreign Minister announced that his Iranian counterpart, Javad Zarif, had invited him to Tehran, and Germany's Economy Minister announced a 60-person business delegation to travel to Tehran within the week. In mid-January 2016, just as the EU lifted its sanctions on Iran in accordance with the JCPOA, Iranian President Hassan Rouhani led a delegation to Europe that signed a reported $22 Billion in business contracts with European entities spanning several industries, in the space of two days.

Thus, while Europe and the US hold many foreign policy perspectives in common relating to Iran, the very different US and

European experiences in the commercial realm following the lifting of nuclear-related sanctions indicates a not insignificant difference in the respective American and European sensitivities to the idea of politically bolstering the ayatollahs of Tehran.

The Arab States

Much of the political and military activity presently underway in the Middle East is commonly attributed by analysts to a geopolitical contest for primacy between Iran and the Arab Gulf led by Saudi Arabia. While there is no doubt that this proposition fairly explains much of the rhetoric and maneuvering involving these two regional powers, the Western tendency to focus on military activity may be missing the more important dimension of the rivalry.

Following the September 24, 2015 stampede at Mecca, Saudi Arabia that killed at least several hundred, and reportedly as many as 2,400, religious pilgrims, the majority of them from Iran, President Rouhani preceded his formal speech to the UN General Assembly on September 28, 2015 by referring to the "old, young, men and women who had come together in the grand and global spiritual gathering of the Hajj, but unfortunately fell victim to *the incompetence and mismanagement of those in charge*." (Emphasis added)

With respect to 'those in charge,' Rouhani continued, "Due to their *unaccountability*, even the missing cannot be identified and **the expeditious return of the bodies of the deceased to their mourning families has been prevented.**" (again emphasis added) The "unaccountability" of "those in charge" was, of course, a veiled reference to the House of Saud, whose King carries as his formal title "The Custodian of the Two Holy Mosques." It is no exaggeration to assume that the Saudi leadership took these words to be an attack on their legitimacy, a subversive message implying a wish for regime change in the Kingdom.

The following summer, on July 9, standing before an estimated 100,000 spirited opponents of the Iranian regime at the annual National Council of Resistance of Iran rally, former Saudi Intelligence Minister and Ambassador to the UK and US, HRH Prince Turki bin Faisal al Saud, called for regime change in Iran – a goal he repeatedly said the Iranian people shared. Pledging support to Maryam Rajavi, head of the Paris-based resistance organization that has long embraced gender equality, women's empowerment and a modern, tolerant practice of Islam, Prince Turki said, "your aim to rid your people of the cancer that is Khomeini is an historic epic and…it will remain inscribed in the annals of History."

Prince Turki described the rise of Ayatollah Khomeini critically, citing interference and threats to neighboring Arab states, and concluding that the fundamentalist regime had broken with the tradition of historic collaboration between Persians and Arabs, depriving the Iranian people of the kind of leadership they had sought after the Shah's demise, and ultimately deepening Iran's isolation. Citing a litany of offenses against the Arab states and people by Iran under Khomeini and his successor as Supreme Leader Ayatollah Khamenei, Prince Turki referred to "its policy of interference based on its insistence and perseverance in founding sectarian organizations and illegal armies in the name of Islam to serve the interests of the leadership in Iran."

There is no question that the Qods Force and Islamic Revolutionary Guard Corps – both organizations created explicitly to protect and perpetuate the religious authority of the Supreme Leader (*Velayat e faqih* or "Guardianship of the Islamic Jurist" under the constitution instituted by Ayatollah Khomeini in 1979) – are heavily engaged in combat operations in Iraq and Syria, and provide essential support to the Houthi fighters that took control of Yemen's seat of government in September of 2014.

These paramilitary forces are not equivalent to the military organizations in most countries. Iran has a national army separate from the IRGC, the Islamic Republic of Iran Army, whose mission is to defend the territory and sovereignty of the state. The IRGC and its elite element the Qods Force are more properly understood as extensions of a Shi'a caliphate, envisioned by Khomeini as a boundless religious domain including but not limited to the sovereign territory of Iran, with both answerable to his divinely-vested constitutional power. The distinction between agents of a sovereign country and agents of a self-appointed religious empire could be relevant to anti-terrorist designations aimed at "non-state" entities which are not privileged by sovereign purposes and duties.

While western governments have, understandably, focused on Iran's long record of terrorist attacks and support for violent non-state actors conducting terrorist activities, it is the religious misconduct of the fundamentalist enterprise spawned by a deeply ambitious cleric with grand visions of unprecedented power that animates the leaders of the Arabian Gulf countries. Islam underpins the legitimacy of leadership in all the GCC countries as well as Jordan, whose Hashemite leaders trace their lineage to the Prophet.

Not only do the Gulf States object to the armed destabilization of Arab states and the inflaming of sectarian hatred led by Iran, they are even more concerned by two forms of hostile action that may be less visible in the West. First is the alleged effort by Iranian agents to support seditious activity in majority Shi'a communities inside Arab states including Bahrain and Saudi Arabia. The fact that Iran exercises major influence in Iraq's majority Shi'ite community, and is overtly fighting to maintain Shi'a-related (Alawite in Syria, Zaidi in Yemen) clients in power in Damascus and Sana'a, is consistent with claims that it is promoting sectarian interests throughout the Arab world, which is predominantly Sunni.

The second and potentially most important form of hostile action by Iran is the effort to shore up the diminishing regional religious influence of the *faqih* himself, the Supreme Leader of Iran. The fact is that since Ayatollah Khomeini's death in 1989, the prestige and followership of the Supreme Leader within Shi'a Islamic communities has declined. The author has described elsewhere how Ayatollah Khamenei was selected by Khomeini as his successor only after a far more senior and respected cleric, the Grand *Marja* Ayatollah Montazeri, displeased him by openly challenging Khomeini's order to execute 30,000 dissident political prisoners – a crime against humanity that has gained political salience recently as audio recordings of Montazeri chastising senior clerics for blackening their historic reputation have been made public.

The author has additionally described elsewhere the thesis derived from regime writings that Ayatollah Khamenei pushed for a nuclear weapons program not as a necessary measure to defend Iran so much as a way to compensate for his deficient religious charisma in the Muslim world. The reality is that in Iraq, the venerated Shi'ite cleric Ayatollah Sistani does not accept the religious authority of Iran's Supreme Leader. The same can be said for many Shi'ite religious authorities in the Arab world; as has been noted, Hizballah in Lebanon is entirely funded by Iran, and hence is not a valid indicator of religious influence.

What will happen when the aging Ayatollah Khamenei passes from the scene? Iran's Arab neighbors recognize that the opportunity for the Iranian regime to elevate a third Supreme Leader would be exploited for maximum effect in the Muslim world, as a potential means of increasing Tehran's leverage over neighboring country populations via religious channels and media. The final period of Ali Khamenei's tenure, therefore, may be the most opportune time to organize Arab Shi'ite clergy in opposition to the Iranian *Velayat e faqih* claim of supreme authority.

The stakes are very high in Iraq in particular. At least three significant Sunni tribes share family ties spanning from central Arabia north to Mosul. For the Saudi royal family, Iraq's Sunni tribes are not foreign neighbors, but blood relatives. Saudi Arabia has re-engaged in Iraq recently at more senior levels than had been used for over a decade. From the Saudi perspective, the prospective passing of Iraq's greatly respected Shi'ite *Marja*, Ayatollah Ali al-Sistani, who will be 87 years of age in August 2017, is of fundamental importance.

As Sistani has resisted Iran's attempts to exercise religious hegemony over southern Iraq, his departure is expected to trigger a major Iranian regime effort to establish dominion over the holy cities of Najaf and Karbala, both of which represent more sacred sites of Islam than any of Iran's shrines. It is a matter of long-term national security concern to Saudi Arabia, and likely many of its neighboring Arab states, that Iran's fundamentalists not breathe new life into a declining – one could say failed – caliphate after the authority of Ayatollah Sistani is no longer there to maintain a barrier.

Just as Saddam Hussein's regime in Iraq was seen by some American security analysts, incorrectly in retrospect, as a major obstacle to a more cooperative and secure Middle East order, now Iraq looms a second time as a lynchpin of the region's future, except in this case, the salient factors are tribal and religious, hence all but unseen through the lenses of western democratic governments. The only common thread is that both communities share a deep concern that the heirs of Khomeini not be further empowered to threaten regional stability and undermine shared interests.

The United States – Pivoting, Tilting, and in Search of Lost Leverage

It is not gratifying for a former US official whose inclination is to promote policies that offer improved prospects for success, to critique policies that have fallen short of success. However, history will likely conclude that President George W. Bush's 2003 Iraq intervention, whether justified at the time or not, suffered from failure to mobilize sensible plans and adequate resources to help restore stability and security as the Iraqi citizenry began their national life post-Saddam. The consequences were grave.

One consequence was that Bush's successor, President Barack Obama, came to office in 2009 determined to extricate US military forces from their extended operations in Iraq and Afghanistan for nearly a decade following the terrorist attacks of September 11, 2001. Obama's precipitous withdrawal of combat forces from Iraq is seen as having created a vacuum that allowed the Islamic State, or Daesh, to establish a successful foothold in Iraq as well as Syria, with adverse consequences that continue in 2017. Mr. Obama promoted a strategic "pivot" to Asia, signaling a diminution of America's strategic appetite to invest further in stabilizing the Middle East.

Adding to the perceptions of declining American interest in the region, the Obama Administration appeared content with the removal from power of Egypt's President Hosni Mubarak, and readily engaged in technical assistance programs with the Muslim Brotherhood-oriented regime of Mohammed Morsi, before large-scale protests against Morsi's anti-democratic leanings led to his stepping down in what some Egyptians termed a "popular impeachment."

Longstanding Arab allies of the US reacted negatively to the perception that decades of cooperation by Mubarak had earned him no American 'loyalty' as he was driven from power. Iranian citizens, in contrast, may have drawn hope and inspiration from the example set by peaceful protestors in both Tunisia and Egypt in what became known as the Arab Spring. Iranians had, after all, exercised the power of protest numerous times, in 1979 as the Shah's regime collapsed; in June 1981 as Khomeini's fundamentalist regime banned political activism led by Mujahedin-e Khalq (MEK) leader Massoud Rajavi and impeached popularly-elected President Abolhassan Bani-Sadr; in 1999 as student protestors were attacked and reportedly thrown from buildings by regime enforcers; and in 2009 as people took to the streets in protest of President Ahmadinejad's falsified re-election vote tally and were met by lethal force.

As if the chaos from President Bush's mishandling of the aftermath of regime change in Iraq and President Obama's seeming abandonment of American commitments to uphold a stable order in the Middle East were not disturbing enough to regional allies, the Obama Administration's Iran diplomacy and accompanying failure to take any measures to arrest the spiraling catastrophe in Syria created major doubts throughout the Middle East regarding the direction and guiding principles of US policy.

When the JCPOA was presented to the US Senate in the summer and fall of 2015, President Obama and Secretary of State John Kerry were at pains to explain that the concessions to Iran were justified because the sole focus of the entire negotiating effort had been to avert a dangerous crisis precipitated by Iran reaching the threshold of producing a nuclear weapon. This was a distortion of the recent past: President Obama had made clear in his speech to the UN General Assembly on September 24, 2013 his belief that "if we can resolve the issue of Iran's nuclear program, that can serve as a major step down a long road towards a different relationship, one based on mutual interests and mutual respect."

To be sure, the P5+1 nuclear accord with Iran was an arms control agreement, one that diminished the prospect of near-term military conflict and one that American nuclear nonproliferation experts had hoped to see for decades. But it was more than those things: the overture by President Obama was an offer to explore the possibility of détente between Washington and Tehran. A generation of US Foreign Service officers, stung by the lingering trauma of the 1979 Tehran Embassy takeover and holding of American hostages, has spent the intervening 38 years hoping for a turn of events that could restore diplomatic relations with a major country, and return Persian studies and Farsi language training to the core competencies of the State Department.

With a circle in power holding the dubious distinctions of being the world's leading state sponsor of terrorism, the leading state in per capita executions of its citizenry, and the principal defender of a leader in Damascus guilty of massive war crimes against innocent civilians, the perceived Obama "tilt" toward Iran raised questions that are still not answered. Does the US not stand with its traditional allies? Does the US not object to Iran's active destabilization of neighboring states, including Iraq, where so many US soldiers were killed or wounded in order to relieve Iraq from dictatorial and violent rule? Is there still a US policy in the Middle East?

As the Administration of President Donald Trump settles into office, answers to these questions are taking two forms. Respected senior cabinet appointees, including former General and now Secretary of Defense James Mattis as well as former ExxonMobil CEO and now Secretary of State Rex Tillerson, have signaled a continuity of solidarity and cooperation with traditional Arab allies including Saudi Arabia. At the same time, early signals from the Trump White House have made clear that far from pursuing a rapprochement with Iran, the US under Mr. Trump will maintain the American commitment to the JCPOA but be vigilant in resisting Iranian provocations.

As this is written, the Trump administration is reinforcing its military capabilities on the ground in both Iraq and Syria, and indication that a more coherent policy is probably forming among the national security team, which also includes the recently-appointed National Security Advisor, Army Lieutenant General H.R. McMaster, the heads of the National Intelligence Directorate and the CIA, the Chairman of the Joint Chiefs of Staff, and the Commander of US Central Command covering the Middle East region. Together, these predominantly military officials have extensive knowledge and experience in the Middle East, and a reputation for strategic thinking and planning. They also share a well-informed aversion to Iran's malevolent role.

The Iranian Resistance – National Council of Resistance of Iran, including the Mujahedin-e Khalq

Experts on Iranian affairs will point to a number of groupings of mostly exiled Iranians, each of which could be characterized as opponents of the regime. With a population of 79 million and a culture that has long been noted for scientific achievement and respect for education, Iranians are a sophisticated and politically-aware people. This was clear in 1980 after the Shah had departed, as Iranians representing every region, minority, gender and political stripe embraced the opportunity to campaign for elected office.

What Iranians learned, to their dismay, only after welcoming Ayatollah Khomeini back from exile as a symbol of nationalist resistance to Communism and western materialism, was that Khomeini's burning ambition was not on behalf of his fellow citizens' sovereignty and political rights, but rather on behalf of his own limitless ambitions for personal power and authority. An intellectually vibrant culture's desire to exercise political rights without fear – already delayed for a generation after nationalist Prime Minister Mossadegh was deposed in a CIA-led coup and the Shah returned to the Peacock Throne in August 1953 – would be crushed a second time, by Khomeini's fundamentalist regime enforcers, in June 1981.

To this day, the deep-seated aspirations of Iranians to control their affairs remain denied by a brutal dictatorship that fears free dialogue and uncensored media more than it fears foreign invasion. The Islamic revolutionary government imposed a cruel sequel to the Shah's repressive and corrupt reign, during which dissenters faced brutal punishment by the dreaded SAVAK security service. Indeed, the initial revolutionary stirrings of public sentiment for representative democracy date back to more than a century ago, in 1906, when Iran's first constitution Parliament were created. Both came under extreme pressures and were thereafter subordinated to the Pahlavi Dynasty.

In 2009, people took to the streets in defiance of the corrupted election results favoring a second presidential term for Mahmoud Ahmadinejad against his rival Mir Hossein Mousavi. The Green Movement, as it was called, sought more than mere election, demanding regime change. It drew international attention to the prospect that outside dissidents could possibly mobilize popular protest sufficient to drive the regime from power. Upon his election in 2013, President Rouhani promised to release Mousavi along with former Speaker of the Parliament Mehdi Karroubi from house arrest within a year – a pledge he has not honored four years later.

There is, in sum, a rich history of modern Iranian pressure for democratic governance in some form. Many colorations of political views have been seen among the regime's internal critics – some who emerged from inside the regime, and others in varying degrees of disaffection with the record of clerical rule. To listen to any of these critics is to hear very similar condemnations of the various misdeeds by a regime that commands no respect among exiled Iranians.

No group has held a more critical view of dictatorial rule in Iran, sustained it longer, actively resisted dictatorship more forcefully, paid a higher price for its opposition, articulated a more coherent and plausible future vision for a post-fundamentalist and democratic Iran, more robustly communicated its defiance of the mullahs' repression to the population inside Iran, or mobilized more exiles and foreign supporters regularly to denounce the Tehran regime, than the National Council of Resistance of Iran (NCRI) which includes the MEK.

The author has, since 2011, independently researched the most credible facts behind familiar allegations commonly repeated in reference to the MEK, and the picture that has emerged from this research is of a proud and independent group of educated Iranians seeking a more just and democratic society, whose refusal to accept repressive and corrupt rule under the Shah led to the execution of most original members by the early 1970s. Those who continued the cause under surviving leader Massoud Rajavi after the revolution soon encountered a wall of brutal repression by Ayatollah Khomeini's regime enforcers, and those dissidents who had not been killed or jailed escaped to life in exile.

Iranians living for nearly 40 years under clerical rule have endured a highly controlled and propagandistic domestic information environment, casting the MEK as traitors when they gained refuge within Iraq under Saddam Hussein's rule during the 1980s Iran-Iraq conflict. While the MEK took up armed resistance against regime targets between 1981 and 2001, the government distorted and embellished this activity by attributing to the resistance controversial and indiscriminate attacks of violence for which no MEK attribution has ever been demonstrated or claimed.

Tehran's diplomats repeatedly leveraged acts like the taking of French and American hostages in Lebanon during the 1980s, and the surreptitious pursuit of a nuclear weapons capability, offering potential cooperation as an inducement to Western governments if they would formally designate the MEK and NCRI as foreign terrorist organizations. By placating Tehran and officially designating the exiled resistance as terrorists starting in 1997, the US and other western democracies placed their intelligence and security organs at the service of Iran's notorious Ministry of

Intelligence and Security in the latter's quest to silence its political opposition.

In 2017, five years since court challenges in the EU, UK, France and the US confirmed the absence of corroboration for the terrorist designations of the NCRI and MEK and formally removed them all, mainstream perceptions of this global network of regime opponents have evolved considerably. No longer do credible voices in the West reflexively repeat the discredited allegations against the resistance. Those who do may be motivated by concern that the nuclear agreement could be abandoned. Others may be slow to accept that long-believed information is unreliable.

In addition to maintaining a coherent, organized, active and forward-looking focal point for exiled Iranians and influential supporters from many countries, the NCRI has been an island of refuge and resilience for the surviving members, families and friends of the tens of thousands of men, women and children jailed, tortured and executed by either the Shah's enforcers or the clerical regime. The NCRI and MEK have followed a remarkable path through a half century of resistance, a path marked by sustained sacrifice and courage that will be remembered by history.

The inward focus and mutual commitment within this society of survivors has been exemplified by the nearly 4,000 who built their own city at Camp Ashraf in Iraq starting in 1986, becoming isolated and endangered after US forces departed Iraq in 2009, and braving seven lethal attacks staged by troops and militias at Iran's behest, until 2016 when the last of the remaining 3,200 were relocated to safety in Albania.

The hesitation among some Iranians in exile to engage with the MEK out of fear of legal recriminations in their host countries, reprisals against their family members in Iran, or jeopardy of their ability to conduct business with Iranian entities had affected the potential for unity among critics abroad. The uniquely amazing life experience of this dedicated society of men and women has, understandably, separated and even alienated them from other exiled Iranians who may hold similar aspirations for change in Iran. Decades of effective isolation from so many other Iranians remains a future challenge as the resistance seeks to broaden international understanding of, and support for, a unified policy confronting Tehran's rulers on moral, religious and political grounds.

No group more closely follows and documents the deception, hypocrisy, corruption and abuses of the mullahs, and their failure to uphold even a basic social contract with the citizens of Iran. While ISIS and the Taliban commit shocking atrocities and destroy world heritage sites in the name of religion, the modern, gender-equal NCRI conducts cordial diplomacy with political and religious notables from around the world. Unlike any other group that has ever been labeled terrorist, the NCRI produces thoroughly-researched and well-written tomes on topics of strategic importance such as the locations, troop numbers, commanders, proxy fighters, casualties and costs of Iran's military operations in Syria. In 2017 the NCRI published a detailed primer on the financial network controlled by the IRGC.

As Western policymakers and analysts call for Muslims to more actively defend their own religion against extremist interpretations, resistance leader Maryam Rajavi has done just that, publishing a cogent rebuttal to those inciting violence in the name of Islam, an essay drawing on the Koran and Islamic teachings to dispel the notion that killing innocents and attacking other faiths is a religious duty. One searches in vain for other examples of accused terrorists, particularly in the Middle East, whose message for years has been to promote religious tolerance, separation of church and state, political legitimacy derived from the ballot box, gender equality and rights for all, and a non-nuclear Iran.

It is not unreasonable to predict that the resistance will soon outlive the defamatory allegations and propaganda wrongly attached to their history, and gain acceptance as a valued resource for governments, including the United States, whose patience with Tehran's criminal vandalism of the international order may finally be running out.

The Iranian People

For an outsider who is not an expert on Persian affairs to presume to enlighten others about the people living in Iran is fraught with risk. Yet, to discuss perceptions of many interested parties regarding the history and future of this important country without considering its own people would, one fears, be the greater injustice. For if justice informs the growing international desire to see a change in Iran that would allow for political legitimacy, transparent governance, guaranteed rights, rule of law and due process, and an end to the long nightmare of judicial abuse, corruption and external aggression, surely it is the citizens of Iran whose wishes must be respected above all.

For many years, one has heard analysts of Iranian affairs in Washington confidently assert that the clerical regime enjoys broad popular support. Many of these analysts took a keen interest in the possibility of curbing Supreme Leader Ali Khamenei's hardline influence when the so-called Green Movement attracted attention during the 2009 uprisings. These same observers have encouraged policymakers to hope that so-called "reformist" figures like President Rouhani hold the potential of transforming Iran's behavior from a serial international outlaw and threat to a normal state that accommodates international law and norms.

History has not been kind to these analysts, and certainly in Washington one will not find much traction for views anticipating that the mullahs will transform the manner in which they exercise power, even less so after the death in January 2017 of the leading "reform" figure, former President Hashemi Rafsanjani.

Thirty-eight years of professed hatred of the exiled resistance, relentlessly echoed through state-controlled media, has most foreign analysts persuaded that the NCRI and MEK enjoy no meaningful support in Iran. The NCRI, by contrast, broadcasts Farsi television programming via satellite and finds viewers surreptitiously telephoning in contributions to its periodic telethons from all over Iran; it also receives continuous videotaped acts of protest staged at recognized sites in Iran.

These indicators of support are understandably rare, since the regime incarcerates, tortures and executes citizens for the simple crime of harboring sympathy for the NCRI. Among the information reaching the NCRI is videotaped footage of regime tanks crushing scores of confiscated satellite dishes, and photographs of equipment emitting powerful jamming signals from elevated sites including the top of Tehran's Milad Tower.

The reason for the regime's near-obsession with the NCRI is that, unique among regime opponents, the NCRI has always rejected Khomeini's brand of Islam. By daring to defy the core of the fundamentalist Islamic enterprise, insisting that Islam is tolerant, peaceful and consistent with the life of modern, educated men and women exercising self-determination, the NCRI threatens the heart of the revolutionary government's claim to power in Tehran.

There are polling organizations in the US that claim to be able to profile the opinions of the Iranian people. Under such conditions of state coercion, such a claim is not credible. The fact is that Iranians do their best to live happy lives under the constraints of the revolutionary government. The authorities cannot prevent news from escaping the country about young people being punished for fraternizing between the sexes, or for posting western-inspired music and dance videos. One can see footage of demonstrations by striking teachers or pensioners suffering from low purchasing power. There are continuous indicators that younger Iranians, including children of senior clerics, indulge in Western-style luxury and ignore religious taboos.

Does this mean that the regime is riddled with corruption and hypocrisy? That Iran's youth aspire to live more freely as others of their generation do even in predominantly Muslim societies? That large segments of the population are discontented due to rampant corruption and diversion of state resources to disrupt political transitions in neighboring countries?

Of course, no definitive answers to these questions can be given so long as the people of Iran are denied any means of political participation.

Conclusion

For a group with so many accumulated violations of international norms, so many transgressions against neighboring states and the international order generally, and the blood of so many principled opponents of religious dictatorship on its hands, the Tehran regime has achieved remarkable success in preventing all who should be its critics from forging a unified view and, most importantly, a unified response. Today we find western governments pondering the implications of a Russian leadership circle utilizing secretive methods of deception, disinformation and suppression of dissent, and Asian countries contemplating a rising China that seeks to lead new multilateral trade and finance institutions. Yet Iran, too, merits global attention as a disruptive actor that has exhibited an impressive ability over a considerable period to control a large population and deflect pressures to change.

Veteran policymakers will say that Western governments have been resolute in condemning Iran's bad behavior and imposing sanctions that brought the Iranians to the nuclear negotiating table. They might also reflect the view that President Rouhani, Foreign Minister Mohammad Javad Zarif, and the Parliament – the most visible Iranian actors one sees in the international media – represent the core of Iran's government, and that more secretive entities including the IRGC, Qods Force, Guardian Council and Expediency Discernment Council represent hard-line tendencies of lesser political importance.

By now, as the hand of these paramilitary forces has been more fully exposed in Syria, Iraq, Yemen and elsewhere, and as the Supreme Leader's religious foundations along with the IRGC have been estimated by Reuters to control as much as 80 percent of Iran's economy, it is no longer possible to view anyone other than the *Velayat e faqih* – the Supreme Leader and the instruments of his direct authority – as the center of power in Iran.

President Obama told the UN in 2013 that President Rouhani, in his June 2013 election, had "received from the Iranian people a mandate" to pursue a moderate course. The reality is that for more than 20 years, fewer than 2 percent of individuals who registered to run for President have been allowed on the ballot after loyalty vetting by the Guardian Council. The vote electing Hassan Rouhani only had 8 of 686 registered candidates on the ballot. The only mandate Rouhani has since followed has been to achieve a nuclear accord that preserves Iran's future rights to become a nuclear weapons state. That mandate came solely from the Supreme Leader, for whom Rouhani had previously served as a nuclear negotiator.

Human rights organizations continuously sound the alarm at the relentless pace of executions in Iran. Suspicion is widespread among resistance families that regime authorities are closely monitoring suspected dissident behavior, and pulling people from their homes without even a judicial process. Others may say that Iran is deeply concerned about the social threat of drug use and that many of those executed are engaged in drug trafficking. The population almost certainly would not receive media reports such as the German Deutsche Welle report on January 18, 2017 that two trucks belonging to the IRGC had been apprehended transiting Germany with a reported 150 kilos of heroin.

Can the international community compare notes and forge a more coherent, common position that demands an end to Iranian meddling in its neighbors' affairs and to the epidemic of executions at home? Can Iran's Muslim neighbors make clear that any successor "Supreme Leader" after Ali Khamenei's passing will receive no homage from Shi'ite clerics outside of Iran? Can the world's democracies come together and make clear that farcical staging of elections allowing only hand-picked loyalists are damaging to democracy everywhere and will be condemned? Can governments pool their resources and compile dossiers on leading regime figures in Iran to hold them accountable at The Hague or the ICC for atrocities such as the 1988 massacre of 30,000 political prisoners?

The fact is that every constituency discussed above has witnessed, and most have endured, Tehran's unceasing international provocations over the years. These include embassy seizures, terrorist attacks, assassinations of regime opponents on the streets of foreign capitals, hostage-takings, mining of the Persian Gulf, arming and funding of terrorist militias, waging of sectarian war against Sunni populations in Iraq and Syria, illicit trafficking in weapons along with human trafficking, and serial violations of other international laws, conventions and norms necessary to the maintenance of a stable international order. By now there can be no disagreement that Iran's revolutionary government since 1979 has imposed a heavy burden on the world.

What is lost when there is no recourse and no relief from this burden is more than the oppression of a great people, large numbers of whom can never return to their beloved country under its present leadership. The countries of the Middle East cannot stabilize hostilities and enable political processes to forge accepted political arrangements. Europe and the United States are torn as they engage in commerce with Iran because they recognize that profits are sustaining the regime's harmful behavior.

The time may finally have arrived when the regime's ability to portray itself in an innocent and sympathetic light will no longer find a credulous audience in the world, when its decades of deceptions have finally been unmasked and recognized as hostile behavior, implicating western governments in its own improprieties. Iran has pushed its neighbors, the major democracies, and one imagines, its own citizens too far, and for too long.

What is the solution? The resistance and its supporters advocate change from within, a resurgence of popular protest in Iran demanding that the clerics step down. Exactly such a scenario materialized in June of 1981, as massive demonstrations across the country stood in opposition to religious dictatorship; the mullahs literally shot their way to power, suppressing the unfulfilled goals of the 1979 revolution and imposing what one scholar described as a "reign of terror."

Having seen the chaos in Iraq and Libya following the collapse of dictatorial regimes there, and the uncertain path in Egypt after Mubarak's removal, governments will be nervous about the prospects for stability in the event of regime collapse in Iran. Could the regime, as a measure to forestall its demise, remove the divine writ of *Velayat e faqih* from the constitution? In that event, there would be no Supreme Leader and no Guardian Council hand-picking candidates for office.

These questions can never be answered with certainty. Events will take their course. But as much as one might fear the uncertainties of an end to religious tyranny in Iran, a consensus is surely growing around the world that the status quo is no longer tolerable. To reclaim the primacy of universal norms and principles in Middle Eastern affairs; to allow for stabilization, reconciliation and reconstruction in a region that has suffered devastating hostilities of late; to give the traditional authorities of Islam an opportunity to reclaim their religion from extremists; and to end, once and for all, the toxic fusion of religious and political authority initiated by Khomeini and imitated by ISIS, it is necessary for the international community to stand united and demand that Iran's regime cease its destructive actions, or face comprehensive action to compel that result.

At last, radical forces have lost their momentum, and stakeholders of international peace and security have recognized the folly of passivity and accommodation. There is a new recognition that peace will only come when justice is upheld. The tide of history will restore Iran to its people.

Ambassador Lincoln Bloomfield served in a number of administrations including as the assistant secretary of state for political military affairs from 2001 to 2005

The inextricable contradiction
between politics and economy in Iran

Mohammad Amin

Introduction

Iran is going through a period we could call transient and is experiencing a trend that has no precedent in the last three decades. The presidential election on May 19, 2017 will have important consequences for Iran's political direction. With Donald Trump in the White House, a new policy is on the horizon for Iran that is likely to establish quite different relations than existed with the two previous US presidents. In the wings of Iranian politics, crucial negotiations are in progress to appoint the successor to the current Supreme Leader, who is suffering from poor health; additionally, this will have profound repercussions on the Iranian political chessboard. Lastly, the conflicts ongoing in Iraq, Syria and Yemen, in which the Iranian regime is a major player, are arriving at decisive turning points that could hurt the regime internally.

What are the prospects for the economy of a country confronted with such stakes? And, above all, what conditions will allow safe investment in such a country? This paper seeks to answer that question with reference to political and social developments on the Iranian scene. We will notably try to understand the direction in which the Iranian leadership is heading. Because economic openness or confinement, political stability or instability, and the opaqueness or transparency of practices are all clues to the direction the regime will take in this new situation.

From this viewpoint, the nuclear agreement signed in July 2015 between Tehran and the P5+1 group is of particular importance. This agreement enabled the lifting of a large number of international sanctions imposed on Iran because of its military nuclear program, which was judged illicit. It is therefore natural to expect the Iranian economy to move towards more openness and stability. The most restrictive aspect of the sanctions was the ban on Iran's use of the international banking transaction system (Swift), prompting Tehran to resort to money-laundering operations using a sophisticated smuggling scheme. UN Security Council Resolution 2231, adopted in July 2015, superseded the six previous resolutions on sanctions against Iran. However, the sanctions imposed by the United States (notably by the Congress, the White House and the Treasury) continue to be applied in accordance with the principle that it is not dependent neither on the nuclear deal nor on Security Council resolutions.

For the Iranian authorities, the pursuit of American sanctions contravenes the nuclear agreement, which led it to express its discontent and to affirm that these sanctions hamper its economic development. But the truth is quite different. Firstly, the lifting of sanctions by the Security Council removed the ban on trade with Iran, which enabled it to reach, in less than a year, about the same level of oil production as before the start of sanctions in 2012. Secondly, the degree to which US sanctions can impact the Iranian economy depends primarily on the internal and regional political leadership taken by Tehran. Also, the appetite of the big American companies to profit from investments in the oil and aeronautics sectors and the promising Iranian market is strong enough to push back the sanctions, if Tehran decides to make the right choices by renouncing its aggressive and destabilizing policies in the Middle East, which are stifling the Iranian political scene.

It can be concluded that since the external factor (international sanctions) which could disrupt the natural course of Iranian politics and economy has virtually disappeared, the current state of the country since 2016 is primarily the result of the Iranian regime's action, based on its interests. This leads us to examine the situation from the perspective of "advancements" and "setbacks". The political and economic progress reflects the general improvement in the situation, leading to a favorable outlook for investments in Iran. The setbacks, however, are the consequences of the tensions and instabilities that make Iran a "risky" country for business and will continue to do so.

Advancements

On June 15, 2016, Iran's oil minister Bijan Zangeneh reported to Parliament that Iranian crude oil production had increased to 3.8 million barrels per day (BPD). On May 6, 2016, the Director General of the National Petroleum Company stated that "crude exports reached 2.1 million BPD". OPEC, which decided, last December in Vienna, to lower production levels has authorized Iran to be exempted from this reduction with the agreement of the Saudis, which has helped increase production in Tehran, enabling it to reach the pre-sanctions level. As a result of this increase, the country's growth rate also jumped.

According to official figures of the Rouhani government, growth in the first six months of the Iranian calendar year 1395 (from March 2016 to March 2017) reached 7.4%. (However, experts doubt this result and consider that the growth in the non-oil sector is so poor that it cannot be said to be a tangible improvement; while the IMF reported in February 2017 that growth in the Iranian economy, for the first half of 2016, was only 0.9%[34]). The inflation rate, which had risen to 40% at the beginning of Hassan Rouhani's term, seems to have declined, according to official estimates, to less than 10%.

For its revival, the Iranian economy has an urgent need for foreign investments and the cooperation of Western companies for the redevelopment of its infrastructure, especially in the oil and transportation industries, and to end the water crisis. Successes have been achieved over the past year in the industrial sector, in particular with the involvement of Renault and PSA in the automotive industry in Iran. Moreover, the purchase of 118 Airbus aircraft could give a new lease on life to the country's worn-out aeronautical fleet.

The visit of numerous foreign trade and diplomatic delegations to Tehran marked a significant starting point for growth in trade. On June 12, 2016, the Ministry of Foreign Affairs published an assessment of these visits: *"In only three months since the beginning of the year, Tehran has hosted six heads of state, two prime ministers, nine MFAs, one High Representative of the EU, one parliamentary president, and one national Vice-President."*

On the political level, since Iran's strategy is to maintain an active presence in the Middle East, its alliance with Moscow on the Syrian issue is perceived as an important strategic achievement. According to the same reasoning, the capture of East Aleppo in December, following ground attacks by the *Pasdaran* (elite IRGC forces) and the Russian Air Force is another major victory for Tehran. However, the outcome of events was not favorable to Tehran, because of the initiatives of Russia and Turkey regarding the Syrian issue.

---

[34] www.imf.org/en/Publications/CR/Issues/2017/02/27/Islamic-Republic-of-Iran-2016-Article-IV-Consultation-Press-Release-Staff-Report-and-44707

Political Nodes

Let's examine the course of events after the nuclear agreement from the political and economic viewpoints. Politically, three important things must be considered: the question of succession of the Supreme Leader, Tehran's involvement in regional conflicts, and the possibility of popular revolts in the country.

1- The question of the succession

It was in the months leading up to the March 2016 legislative elections that the first signs of dissension around the succession of the Supreme Leader emerged. Suffering from health problems, Ali Khamenei himself spoke twice about the need to appoint a successor. Rafsanjani, the influential president of the State Expediency Council, spoke of the advantages of a collegial leadership for the Supreme Leader's office. Ahmad Khatami, an eminent member of the Assembly of Experts (an institution that nominates the Leader), said on January 27: *"Of the seven meetings of the Assembly of the new legislature, five meetings were devoted to the question of the succession of the Leader."* He later explained that several candidates were selected, but that their identity will remain confidential. On March 4, 2016, following the death of Ayatollah Tabasi, a senior dignitary of the regime and director of an important religious institution in Astan Quds Razavi (linked to the mausoleum of the 8th Shia imam in the holy city of Mashhad), Khamenei replaced him with Ebrahim Raisi, who was at the time Attorney General. The latter is a cleric of no high ranking in the Shiite hierarchy, but he is held in special esteem by Khamenei, particularly because of his central role in the massacre of political prisoners in 1988 in Iran. With his appointment to this post, some speculated about Raisi as Khamenei's favorite candidate for his own succession.

In any case, the question of the succession is one of major internal struggle at the top of Iranian power, making this crucial issue a source of tension and instability for the Iranian political climate.

The recent death of Rafsanjani, considered to be the regime's number two and a leader of the so-called reformist faction, has seriously undermined the prospect of a possible appeasement of the political scene. Three days after his death, the official daily newspaper, Sharq wrote about Rafsanjani (January 12, 2017 issue): *"The nuclear agreement (contested) has lost its biggest support in Iran."* This event will not be without effect on the presidential election in May. In the balance of power, the absence of Rafsanjani has diminished the weight of Hassan Rouhani in the system. Consequently, if he is re-elected as President, it is very likely that he will be obliged to be regrettably docile vis-à-vis the Leader. Mohammad Khatami, the "moderate" President in office from 1997 to 2005, was in the same position in his second term. He then described his powerlessness to govern in the following terms: *"I am merely the system's supply man!"*

2- Involvement in regional conflicts

Iran is currently involved in three conflicts in the Middle East. In Yemen, the Ansarullah group, which is affiliated with the Revolutionary Guards, is fighting to preserve the capital Sana'a, receiving arms, money and military instructions from Iran. In Iraq, dozens of Shi'ite extremist groups affiliated with Tehran are taking part in the repression of the Sunni population, while working to dislodge Daesh from its positions. In Syria, the *Pasdaran* are directly engaged with their troops in a murderous war that has caused havoc for six years. Observers are reporting massive human and material investments by the *Pasdaran* in Syria. The financial assistance provided by Tehran to the Assad regime would amount to 2.5 billion dollars per month[35]. The many

---

[35] Regarding Tehran's spending in the war in Syria, which has had a heavy impact on the Iranian economy since 2011, the following information is significant:

extremist militias under the *Pasdaran* in the various countries of the region are financed entirely by the Iranian regime, which is a significant burden on the country's economy. The list of these groups provides a glimpse of the magnitude of the costs:

On May 28, 2013, Adib Mialeh, head of the Syrian central bank, spoke (in the official daily newspaper, Tishreen) of the opening of two lines of credit worth $4 billion by Tehran for the Syrian regime, together with a $3 billion loan.

On August 27, 2013, the French daily, Libération, estimated that "Iran has, up to present, spent about $17 billion in the war in Syria."

On July 8, 2015, the official Syrian news agency, SANA, reported: "Syrian President Bashar al-Assad has approved a law authorizing a credit of the $1 billion from Iran, our major regional ally."

In December 2014, Reuters, quoting a Syrian official who wished to remain anonymous, wrote that if it had not had the support of Iran, Assad's regime would not have survived the crisis. The dispatch adds that, in July of the previous year, Iran granted a credit of $ 4.5 billion to the Syrian regime, the bulk of which is used for the purchase of petrochemical products. (Deutch Welle, January 6, 2015).

On May 3, 2015, the Iranian daily, Sharq, said: "Iran, China and Syria contribute monthly to the payment of $500 million, through the sale of oil and other lines of credit to Syria."

On April 27, 2015, the Christian Science Monitor wrote: "Diplomatic sources in Beirut estimate that Iran spends between $1 billion and $2 billion a month in Syria in cash handouts and military support. Staffan de Mistura, the United Nations envoy to Syria, recently told a private gathering in Washington that Iran has been channeling as much as $35 billion a year into Syria, according to one of the participants at the meeting."

On May 5, 2015, Nazir Hakim, secretary of the political delegation of the opposition Syrian National Coalition, speaking at a conference at the French National Assembly, said: "In my opinion, Assad can not remain in power without Tehran's support. The latter has paid $87 billion out to him over three years. My assertions are supported. Assad will not leave power as long as the Iranian regime does not leave Syria."

Country	Group
Iraq	Badr Organization
	Al-Nujaba Movement
	Asa'ib Ahl al-Haq
	Kata'ib Hezbollah
	Kata'ib al-Imam Ali
	Saraya Al Khorasani
	Kata'ib Sayyid al-Shuhada
	Liwa Abu Fadl
	Liwa'a Zulfiqar
	Harakat al-Abdal
	And about thirty other groups
Yemen	Ansarullah (Houthis)
Lebanon	Hezbollah
Bahrain	Tayyar al-amal al-islami
	Coalition of February 14
Palestine	Islamic Jihad Movement
	Al-Sabirin Movement
Persian Gulf	Gulf Hezbollah
Egypt	Egyptian Republican Guard
Kuwait	Hezbollah of Kuwait
Afghanistan	The Fatemiyoun Brigade
Pakistan	The Zainabiyoun Brigade

Although the Iranian authorities have often mentioned their financial support for these groups, no figures have yet been published. Observers estimate this figure at between 4.5 and 8 billion dollars annually. The expenditure weighs both on the Iranian economy and Iranian politics, and is adding to the instability. Moreover, the opaque nature of these operations, which involve money laundering and embezzlement, is a source of corruption in the country. However, the financial burden of this problem is secondary; the main problem lies in the pressure exerted by these military commitments on the political climate.

Notable are the tensions created with neighboring countries. Today Iran has conflicting relations with Turkey, Saudi Arabia, Bahrain, the UAE ... Tehran's constant efforts to provide weapons for these conflicts, in particular by sending ships, poses a risk of collapse, and of confrontation with Saudi forces or American ships. Moreover, as long as Tehran continues to be involved in these conflicts, it runs the risk of a destabilization if these enterprises fail.

3 – The risks of revolts

Eight years have passed since the post-electoral popular uprising of 2009, a dramatic episode in recent history that shook the theocratic power. The leaders then spoke of the dangers of these revolts for the future of the regime. Yet the virulence of the discontent which was at the origin of these popular movements is far from being appeased. With the worsening of the economic crisis and the growth in poverty and unemployment, this discontent has since been radicalized and deepened.

This discontent emerged once again in February 2017, in the form of massive demonstrations that lasted more than a week in Khuzestan, in the south of the country. The scale of the protest against water and electricity cuts, and severe environmental problems, was so vast that Hassan Rouhani had to go personally to try to calm the tensions. On October 28, 2016, a gathering organized to celebrate the memory of Cyrus the Great, the founder of ancient Iran, quickly turned into a political demonstration that evolved into a huge protest movement against the ruling power. Social movements of workers, teachers, nurses, retired persons, etc., are constantly on the rise in Iran. On February 25, 2017, General Hassan Ashtari, commander of the State Security Forces, said during a speech at the Ministry of the Interior: *"We have 20 to 30 rallies and demonstrations every day across the country, that we need to know how to manage."*[36]

On June 6, 2016, Interior Minister Abdolreza Rahmani revealed at a hearing in Parliament that nearly 600,000 people are being arrested every year across the country[37]. These arrests take place during daily checking operations supported by the *Basij* and *Pasdaran*. In fact, the regime continuously has to run large-scale operations to control society, in order to counter any desire for revolt. Dozens of law enforcement agencies have been set up for this purpose. The following table provides a partial list of these bodies:

---

[36] Basij press agency, February 25, 2007
(http://basijnews.ir/fa/news/8830737/%D8%AC%D9%85%D8%B9-%D8%A2%D9%88%D8%B1%DB%8C-%D8%A7%D8%B1%D8%A7%D8%B0%D9%84-%D9%88-%D8%A7%D9%88%D8%A8%D8%A7%D8%B4-)

[37] The official government site, June 6, 2016
(http://www.dolat.ir/NSite/FullStory/News/?Serv=8&Id=280664)

Domain of Control	Controlling Organization
Popular protests and uprisings	Sarallah camp (Tehran) / Rassoul-Akram camp (Sistan-Baluchistan) / Nasr camp (Kerman) / Fajr camp (South Khorasan) / Mohammad-Rassoul-Allah division (Tehran) / Seyedo-shohada division (Tehran) / 30 divisions in each of the 30 geographical departments / Al-Zahra anti-riot brigade / Ashura anti-riot brigade / Imam-Ali Bassij brigade / NOPO
Communications	Department of Communications and Electronics of the Pasdaran / Central Office for the Surveillance of Telephone Monitoring / Committee for the Fight against Cyber Delinquency / Committee for the Monitoring of Internet Sites / Higher Security Council of the Information Exchange Service / Section Of the Prosecutor's Office dedicated to Internet offenses / Filtering Committee working under the authority of the judiciary / Technical Information Agency / Internet Council of the Basij / Cyberspace Command acting under the authority of the Pasdaran / Cyberspace Army / Army of the Sun / Organized Crime Monitoring Center working under the authority of the Pasdaran / Ministry of Intelligence Technical Branch / Special Internet Offences Tribunal / FATA (cyberspace)
Young adults and women (particularly control over dress)	Anti-Vice Police / Property Order Headquarters / Women's Police / Vice Security Police / Social Police / School Police / Youth Police / Family Police
Universities	Disciplinary Committees / Offices of Representatives of the Supreme Leader / University Security Service / Basij Sections
Workers and employers	Government Department Security Service / Selection Units / Basij sections / Workers Center / Islamic Employment Council

Society	Police backup units / Local Police / Invisible police / Metro Police / Ansar-e Hezbollah / Political commissars of the Pasdaran
The Press	Inspection units of the Ministry of Islamic Guidance / Press control delegation / Special Court of the Press
Clergy	Special Clerical Court / Bureau of statistics on religious seminars in Qom / Imam Dafar Sadegh Brigade
General	Tamin councils (responsible for supplying personnel for security and repression forces in each geographical department / Tamin councils of districts / Social and cultural councils / Office of the Prosecutor of Tehran / Revolutionary Court / 110 police

The careful distribution of tasks between these various organs makes it possible to cover and control the entire social and political life of the population. The incessant activity of these bodies is also reflected in the amount of capital punishment in Iran, a country that holds the world record of per capita executions. The pace of executions is punctuated by the degree of repression that the power wants to exert over society in response to the tensions that affect the system. The number of executions for the Iranian year of 1394 (March 2015 to March 2016) is a strong indicator of the relationship between the increase in executions and the regime's need to increase its control during sensitive periods. The peak of executions was reached in June, with 200 hangings. At a time of great political tension over the signing of the nuclear agreement and the cutback it had to agree to in its nuclear program, the regime increased executions to offset the setback. This was a means of stifling by terror any desire for social advancement, following an agreement perceived as a renunciation of the "unwavering right" which the regime had ceaselessly reiterated for ages.

Executions(March2015 - March2016)

It is clear that the cost of these operations of control and social repression, which amount to nothing less than an open war against the population, is colossal. However, the effect of such a repressive system, beyond the pressures it exerts on the economy, is to create a social powder keg that could explode at any moment, and with intensity. The current desolation of Syria is, in fact, the consequence of the repressive system developed by the Assad clan for many years. Unfortunately, the Iranian power is traveling the same deadly path. The day-to-day operations of control have created a deep instability in the Iranian system.

The economic nodes

In the current state of the country, three important economic factors are causing insecurity for foreign investors: the risk of new international sanctions, the bankruptcy of the Iranian banking system, and the absence of the rule of law.

1- The risk of new international sanctions

With Donald Trump in the White House, we are faced with an administration that considers Tehran as "the biggest state sponsor of terrorism," (James Mattis, US Secretary of State, February 4). Although the new administration has said it does not want to question the substance of the nuclear agreement with Iran, the declared positions of its officials nevertheless give rise to the prospect of new sanctions. The House of Representatives and the Senate have voted almost unanimously to renew sanctions against Iran for another decade. The D'Amato law sanctions countries that invest more than 40 million dollars a year in the Iranian oil sector.

The effects of these sanctions were underlined in a 180-page report produced by a delegation of French parliamentarians who visited Iran. Entitled "The effects of extraterritorial application of US legislation", the report states: "Non-US banks can participate in financing business with Iran provided they do not use a single US dollar, and that no branch of the banks in question is involved in such transactions, and it must be ensured that Iranian natural and legal persons subject to sanctions have no connection with transactions covered by international banks."

Normally, under the pressure of many US companies wanting to take advantage of the promising Iranian market, the US sanctions against Iran should have decreased, or at least should not have increased. This would have been possible on condition that the Iranian authorities had agreed to refrain from further provocations and to engage in a process of detente with their neighbors. The missile test by Tehran in the second week of the Trump administration showed that Tehran intends to maintain its posture of defiance towards the international community. Ballistic tests and the UN Security Council's urgent meeting to examine Tehran's violation of Security Council Resolution 2231 shook the markets in Tehran. This did not prevent the Iranian authorities from reiterating their intention to continue the ballistic tests. In

February 2017, Behnam Ben-Taleblu, an analyst with the Washington-based Foundation for Defense of Democracies, noted with regard to the Iranian program that *"Since the July 2015 announcement of the nuclear deal known as the Joint Comprehensive Plan of Action (JCPOA), Iran has tested as many as 14 ballistic missiles."*[38].

These illegal activities, coupled with the military interference and destabilization of the regime in the Middle East, including its harmful role in Syria, and the financing and shipment of weapons to the Lebanese Hezbollah and the Yemeni Ansarullah, are likely to favor the adoption of new sanctions by the United States. For his part, the Secretary-General of the United Nations, in his report of January 9, 2017, said *"I am very concerned by this statement, which suggests that transfers of arms and related materiel from the Islamic Republic of Iran to Hezbollah may have been undertaken contrary (to a Security Council resolution)"* Such reports can lead to more sanctions by other countries against Tehran, and make it more difficult to do transactions with Tehran.

Another important risk for trade with Iran is the money-laundering. The Financial Action Task Force (FATF) decided on 24 June 2016 to keep Tehran on its blacklist. If it fails to show that it is giving up terrorist financing and laundering activities, the World Anti-Money Laundering Organization may decide, at its next review in June 2017, to impose new restrictions on financial transactions with Tehran. In addition, the Basel Institute of Governance, which indexes countries according to the level of money-laundering risk, rated Iran as a high-risk country for the third consecutive year.[39]

---

[38] http://www.defenddemocracy.org/content/uploads/documents/20917_Behnam_Ballistic_Missile.pdf

[39] http://www.fatf-gafi.org/countries/d-i/iran/documents/public-statement-february-2017.html

2 – Banking system bankruptcy

One important fact that emerged after the lifting of sanctions was the catastrophic state of the Iranian banking system. In December 2016, the Iranian media revealed that Saderat Bank, a major bank in Iran, having made a profit of 420 billion tomans in the first half of the previous Iranian calendar year, suffered a loss of 2,700 billion tomans in the first half of this year.

In January 2017, the shareholders of Melat Bank suffered a loss of 3,000 billion tomans. On 30 January, the Tehran Stock Exchange suffered a shock when the shares of Saham Bank, another major bank, fell by 33%. The media also reported on February 4 that the shareholders of the Tejarat and Melat banks lost more than 4,000 billion tomans in stock market securities in just a few weeks. The publication of this information highlighted the bankruptcy of the banking system, which has suffered for several years from the structural dysfunctionality of the Iranian economy.

The government is avoiding discussing the bankruptcy of banks for fear of political and social repercussions. This has only delayed solutions to correct the system. In June 2016, the parliamentary research center deplored the situation of "insolvency" and "bankruptcy" of the banks and explained in a report: *"In Iranian banks, non-performing loans constitute about 17% of total loans. Compared with neighboring countries, where this is usually a one-digit figure, the rate is very high in Iran."* Difficulties in fulfilling payment obligations have reached worrisome proportions. Payment arrears (over six months) were steadily increasing under the Rouhani government,[40] as is shown in the following table:

40

https://index.baselgovernance.org/sites/index/documents/Basel_AML_Index_Report_20 16.pdf

2013: 67,000 billion tomans

2014: 72,000 billion tomans

2015: 91,000 billion tomans

2016: 100,000 billion tomans

In Iran, the ratio of arrears to total bank loans is 15.4%, while in Europe it is around 4%. In order to understand the state of health of the Iranian banking system, it is also necessary to look at "ambiguous accounts". According to the Minister of Justice, Mostafa Pourmohammadi, *"There are 50 million ambiguous bank accounts with no precise identity ... Such data call into question the banking system of our country[41]"*.

The banking crisis is the result of a defect that has affected the Iranian system for many years. In fact, banks have been converted into credit unions for easy, abusive and illegal loans by affiliates of the Revolutionary Guards and the foundations of the Supreme Leader. Another cause of this crisis is that a considerable part of the banking potential is under the domination of the *Pasdaran*, State Security Forces, the Bassij militia and other bodies serving the Supreme Leader. The table below shows how they took over the banks, dedicating the profits to the financing of the Pasdaran operations for the control of the company and the military commitment in the different countries of the region. The result is that the banking system is incapable of accomplishing its role of supporting investment in the country's production and trade.

---

[41] ILNA official press agency, August 15, 2016

	Bank	Ownership	Number of companies	Number of branches
1	Keshavarzi	Government	7	1928
2	Sepah	Government	4	1754
3	Postbank	Government	1	406
4	Melli	Government	26	3325
5	Export Developmen t Bank of Iran	Government	5	40
6	Bank of Industry & Mine	Government	8	62
7	Tose'e Ta'avon	Government	4	466
8	Maskan	Government	26	1281
9	Refah Kargaran	Government	3	1035
10	Eghtesad Novin		12	262
11	Parsian	Automotive manufacturers, with shareholdings by EIKO and the government	17	293
12	Karafarin	EIKO – (Supreme Leader)	7	106
13	Saman		9	142
14	Pasargad	The *Pasdaran* are shareholders	68	327
15	Sarmayeh		4	153
16	Sina	The Foundation for the Disinherited	3	242
17	City Bank	Tehran City Hall	14	261

18	Day	The Foundation of Martyrs	13	91
19	Middle East		5	13
20	Ansar	Pasdarans	9	626
21	Saderat	Pasdarans are shareholders	10	2706
22	Mellat	EIKO (Supreme Leader) is a shareholder	16	1592
23	Tourism	The Ahmadinejad faction	4	87
24	Qavamin	State security forces	6	721
25	Tejarat	The Pasdarans and the Quds Razavi Foundation	21	2092
26	Iran Zamin	The Pasdarans and the Quds Razavi Foundation	5	356
27	Ayandeh			165
28	Iran Venezuela Bi National Bank			
29	Hekmat	The Army	2	128
30	Mehr Eqtesad	The Basij militia		800
31	Resalat	Pouyesh-Salehine, affiliated with the Pasdarans and Mahan Air Line		282

3 - Absence of the rule of law

The absence of the rule of law in Iran is manifested in a number of areas: the opaque nature of ownership, unpredictable interference in the economy by military and religious bodies, systematic abuses by the authorities with regard to the budget and public property, a lack of legal certainty, and regulatory instability.

Interference by the various organs of power in the economy has taken a formal turn over the last ten years. The religious foundations of the Supreme Leader and the military institutions unlawfully appropriated entire sections of the economy, including thousands of businesses and the bulk of the financial market and stock market. According to a study published by the Foundation for Middle Eastern Studies (FEMO), based in Paris42, the process of domination of the economy by the Supreme Leader has led to the formation of 14 financial, commercial and industrial organizations, as depicted in the following table:

	Military institutions and religious foundations	Other name
1	The Headquarters of the Execution of the Imam's Command	Setad-e Ejraii-e faraman-e Emam (EIKO)
2	The Foundation of the Disinherited	Bonyad-e Mostaz'afan
3	The Holy Domain of Imam Reza	Astan-e Qods-e Razavi, Khorasan province
4	The Foundation of Martyrs	
5	The Assistance Committee	
6	The Cooperative Foundation of the Revolutionary Guards Corps	IRGC
7	The Khatem-ol-anbya headquarters	[Prophet Mohammad] of the Guards Corps (IRGC)
8	The Bassij Cooperative Foundation	The Popular Mobilization Force
9	The Qadir investment company	Affiliated with the Ministry of Defense
10	The Social Security Organization of the Armed Forces	SATA
11	The Khatem-ol-Ossia Headquarters	Affiliated with the Ministry

---

42 http://www.fondationfemo.com/images/femo-2105/Mohammad-Amin.pdf

		of Defense
12	The Cooperative Foundation of the Armed Forces High Command	
13	The Cooperative Foundation of the Police Forces	NAJA
14	The Army Cooperative Foundation	

Investments by these economic organizations are mainly in strategic sectors such as hydrocarbons, mining, communications, petrochemicals, automotive production, banking, insurance and construction. Embezzlement, bribes and other forms of misappropriation of public property result from the absence of the rule of law. They are also the source of financial instability and disorders in economic activity.

Last year, revelations about major corruption cases shook the regime, including the exorbitant pay of bank directors and senior government officials, the uncovering of 63 bank accounts belonging to the head of the judiciary, Sadeq Larijani, reports on the illegal confiscation of public land, and cases of fraud by General Mohammad-Baqer Qalibaf, Mayor of Tehran, as well as other colossal frauds in the teachers' savings fund ... Official reports in this area leave no doubt as to the extent of the problem.

The main instances of corruption in the Iranian economy:

- arbitrary tariffs and unannounced import/export regulations applied to anything and everything;

- the obtaining of exorbitant bank loans by the regime's leaders and companies affiliated to the *Pasdarans*, as well as their transfer to unproductive sectors;

- the organization of bid calls without respect for due legal process;

- the ridiculously low-priced auctioning of public companies to the *Pasdarans* and the Foundations of the Supreme Leader;

- the sale of oil outside the legal framework;

- abusive land speculation and destruction of the country's natural resources.

Unwise decisions, regulatory confusion and the instability of banking policy and the management of financial institutions have increased uncertainties about the Iranian economy. The President of the Confederation for Exports, Mohammad Lahouti, recently stated: *"At present, we have some 1600 conflicting regulations that are weighing on the country's trade (...) Laws that are often in contradiction with each other"*[43].

Obtaining business licenses in Iran requires the approval of 33 different bodies. And when business proves profitable, dozens of bodies, in addition to the General Directorate of Taxes and Social Security, claim shares of the earnings. Successive changes in regulations add to confusion about their application. This situation becomes more complicated with the constant changes to the leadership of directorates. In addition, there are incessant legal reprisals against state and production company directors and administrators. In Iran, political and financial disputes between the factions of power usually end with the sacrificing of these directors and administrators.

Last December, one businessman was sentenced to death, five were sentenced to life imprisonment, and 38 others were sentenced to a total of 841 years' imprisonment. Recently, the director of the bank Melat was arrested by the Revolutionary Guards. In February, the director of the steel industry was imprisoned. On

---

[43] The daily newspaper, Ebtekar (http://www.ebtekarnews.com/?newsid=36068)

February 1, the President of the Court of Auditors announced that proceedings had been instituted against 87 government officials for unacceptable salaries. On February 22, the regime's Attorney General announced that he had handed the ministry a list of about ten directors having dual nationality (illegal in Iran), for possible punishment. Earlier, he had mentioned the cases of three bank directors and the summoning of 140 state officials about their salaries.

Conclusion

In recent months, several foreign companies have announced that they have given up doing business in Iran. Total has set a condition for its involvement in the exploitation of the largest natural gas field in the world that some of the US sanctions should be lifted; Boeing, which has signed an agreement to sell 110 aircraft to Iran, is currently reluctant to implement the project; Japanese Mitsubishi has suspended negotiations for the sale of aircraft; Amazon has announced the suspension of sales to Iran; Scottish bank RBS refused the British government's pressure for cooperation with Tehran; And even Russia has renounced the sale of Sukhoi planes to Iran.[44]

These renunciations are mainly due to concerns raised by new US sanctions. Yet, even if the United States decides not to change its policy vis-à-vis Iran, the problem of the uncertainties inherent in Iran's policy and economy will remain. On the one hand, Tehran's strategy is aimed at maintaining its grip on Iranian society and continuing its interference in the Middle East; on the other hand, the regime wants to work with Western companies to raise the necessary financing for its operations. However, the requirements of this strategy, the use of money laundering, and its

---

[44] Assadollah Askaroladi, President of the Chamber of Commerce of Iran, Russia and China. Sharq daily newspaper, January 8, 2017.

disregard for rule of law create a "risky" climate unfavorable to investment in Iran.

Mohammad Amin is a specialist in political economy, an associate researcher at the Foundation for Middle Eastern Studies (FEMO), author of a report on the control of the Revolutionary Guards over the Iranian economy published by the FEMO.

Iran's Presidential Election and Supreme Leader's Calculus

Ramesh Sepehrrad & Reza Bulorchi

Executive summary

On May 19, 2017, Iran will hold its 12th presidential elections. Although elections in theocratic Iran are neither free nor fair and primarily staged to provide a false show of popular legitimacy and portray Iran as a functioning democracy, they offer an opportunity to measure the regime's political, economic and strategic health index and their trajectory. Elections are also an indicator of the regime's assessment of the gravity of the internal and external threats posed to its survival. Otherwise, elections, as a representation of exercise in democracy in Iran, are devoid of any legitimacy since no real pro-democracy opposition takes part in them.

According to Iran's Constitution, the vali-e-faqih (Supreme Leader) is the ultimate decision maker. The President, although provided many executive authorities, by far plays a second fiddle to the office of the Supreme leader when it comes to national security and foreign policy decisions. The political and ideological standing of Iran's Supreme Leader, Ayatollah Ali Khamenei, however, has been on the demise, particularly since 2009.

The upcoming presidential election is especially significant because it coincides with two major and consequential developments. One is the death of former president, Hashemi Rafsanjani, on January 8, 2017. Rafsanjani was a pillar of the regime and also key to victory of the current president, Hassan Rouhani, in 2013, and his absence is a major blow to Rouhani and his faction as they prepare for the election.

The second development is the end of the "Golden Era" of Obama and the inauguration of the new administration in Washington. The unpredictability and the policy uncertainty, which Tehran associates with the new administration, has created deep confusion in its policy circles. This ambiguity has and will continue to be a source of policy paralysis and paranoia, particularly in the Supreme Leader's office as he plans for the upcoming presidential elections.

Khamenei's 2017 election calculus is based on three imperatives: The first is his fear of an election-triggered popular unrest similar to the 2009 post-election uprisings. The second is his assessment of the international and regional geopolitical conditions in the aftermath of the new U.S. administration. Third, and equally important, is Khamenei's deteriorating health and the issue of succession.

However, the result of Khamenei's calculus and whether he will "engineer" another electoral win for his preferred candidate or reluctantly give the nod to Rouhani, the Islamic Republic of Iran will not move on the path of real reform and moderation since it is inherently and structurally incapable of doing so. Iran's election will be best understood as one held by a regime in fear of its unraveling in the hands of its people, and paralyzed with uncertainty about whether or not the approach of the new U.S. administration will expedite its demise.

Introduction

According to basic principles of democracy, elections are not enough to assure popular sovereignty since dictators often use the resources of the state to tamper with the election process and results. The Iranian President, Hassan Rouhani, claims "elections in Iran are fair, free, democratic, and competitive; critics of Iran's elections should turn to their own election process."[45] Yet, the Iranian political structure is riddled with un-elected bodies with the Supreme Leader at the helm. It lacks real popular sovereignty through free and fair elections and its claims of holding elections as an exercise in democratic practice has no credibility since the real pro-democracy opposition is not a part of it. Hence, casting doubts on such claims by the Iranian President.

The nature of elections in Iran is different than those in democratic countries. In order to understand the elections, one has to briefly study the Iranian Constitution first. Starting with Article 1, which states "The form of government of Iran is that of an Islamic Republic" while Article 2 explains "the necessity of submission to God and the "fundamental role" of "divine revelation" in "setting forth the laws." Iran's flag must contain the phrase "Allahu Akbar" (Article 18) and "Absolute sovereignty over the world and man belongs to God" (Article 56).[46] These articles clearly define Iran as a theocratic state.

Under the section of national sovereignty, the Constitution (Article 57) reads "The powers of government in the Islamic Republic are vested in the legislature, the judiciary, and the executive powers. They operate under the supervision of the absolute authority of the *vali-e-faqih* (Supreme Leader)

---

[45] http://en.mehrnews.com/news/124071/US-Elections-equally-unfair-unhealthy-as-Trump-admits

[46] http://www.worldpolicy.org/blog/2010/10/12/detailed-analysis-iran%E2%80%99s-constitution

command."[47] The role of Supreme Leader as described here defines Iran as an authoritarian state.

The Iranian Constitution acknowledges the formation of the "Guardian Council" (Article 91), which is comprised of six theologians appointed by the Supreme Leader and six jurists appointed by the head of the Judiciary, who himself is appointed by the Supreme Leader. The article reads "With a view to safeguarding the Islamic ordinances and the Constitution and in order to examine the compatibility of the legislation passed by the Islamic Consultative Assembly with Islam, a council to be known as the Guardian Council is to be established." In 1991, the Guardian Council published its interpretation of its role regarding its duty and the elections by stating that the "supervision mentioned in Article 90 of the Constitution is approbative and covers all stages of elections including approval or disqualification of the candidates."[48] The existence of the Guardian Council (Article 93) is a prerequisite for all other bodies. For example, "The Islamic Consultative Assembly (the Parliament) does not hold any legal status if there is no Guardian Council in existence." The Constitution further clarifies (Article 99): "The Guardian Council has the responsibility of supervising the elections of the Assembly of Experts for Leadership, the President of the Republic, the Islamic Consultative Assembly, and the direct recourse to popular opinion and referenda."

In a nutshell, elections in Iran are tightly engineered, supervised, vetted and managed by two un-elected bodies, the Guardian Council and the Supreme Leader. As for the elected officials like the Iranian President, Rouhani, "the Guardian Council also supervises the election process to guarantee its health." In other words, the fragile and vulnerable political structure that

---

[47] http://www.wipo.int/edocs/lexdocs/laws/en/ir/ir001en.pdf

[48] http://ncr-iran.org/en/news/iran-world/19913-iran-election-or-selection-what-are-the-prospects

lacks popular sovereignty requires the Guardians Council to keep it in shape.

Still, every four years, elections take place on national and local levels for presidency, Islamic Consultative Assembly (the Parliament) and City and Village Councils. Additionally, elections for the Assembly of Experts are held every eight years. All candidates have to be approved by the Guardian Council.

The Supreme Leader is the highest ranking political and religious authority in the Islamic Republic of Iran with control over armed forces, the judicial system, state television, and other key governmental organizations. The Supreme Leader is accountable to God and all presidential candidates must state their categorical allegiance to him and have his approval.

Moreover, the Iranian political structure only allows men to reach the highest ranking elected and un-elected bodies. Leaving out an entire gender, structurally unrepresented and undermined, further erodes the claims of "free and fair" elections in Iran.

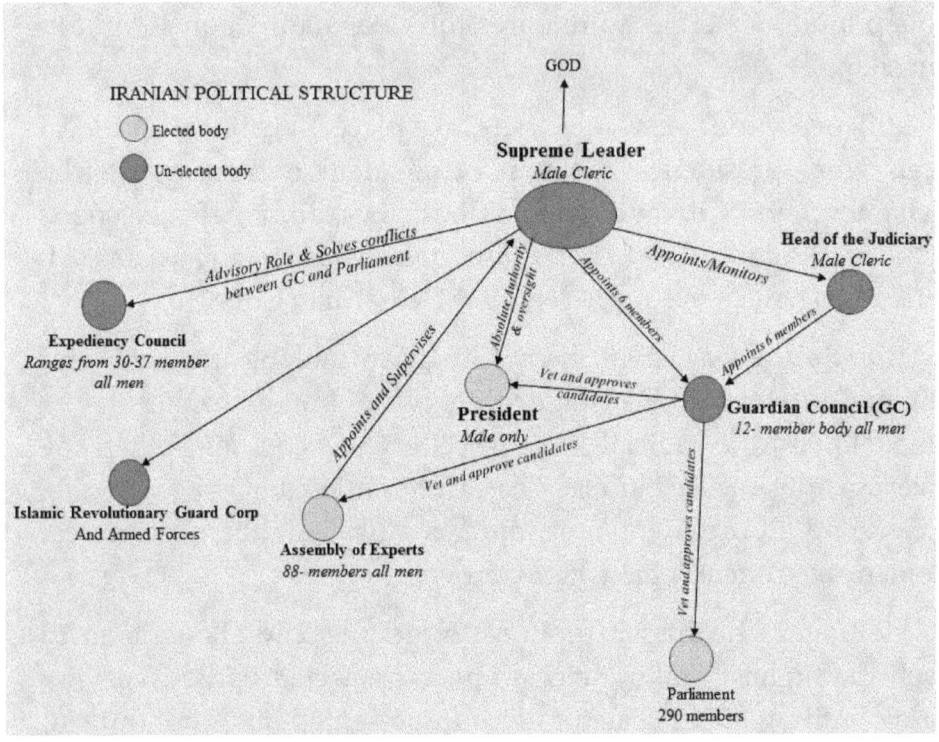

Iran's Supreme Leader

The Islamic Republic is built on the principle of *Velayat-e-faqih*, the Supreme Leadership of a non-elected Ayatollah (the *vali-e-faqih*), who sits at the core of the state's legitimacy and is powered by the Constitution with immense religious, economic and political authority.[49] Iran's entire political and security structure is geared to protect the system of *Velayat-e-faqih*, and ensure its permanence as the prerequisite to all other goals for the state.

Long before coming to power, the founding father of Iran's Islamic Republic, Ayatollah Ruhollah Khomeini, published a book entitled *Velayat-e-faqih*, which provided the general contours of the state's governing doctrine. In his book, Khomeini stresses "there

---

[49] The concept, which literally means the guardianship of the religious jurist, the *vali-e-faqih* is the vice regent to the Mahdi, the messianic Twelfth Imam of Shi'ite Islam.

are no real boundaries between Islamic countries" and that the *Vali-e-Faqih's* authority "to administer the society's affairs is the same as that Prophet Muhammad enjoyed."

To better understand the vast authority of *vali-e-faqih* in practical terms, Khomeini's remarks when at the apex of power in Iran are helpful. In his January-1988 open letter to Ali Khamenei, Iran's then-president and later successor to Khomeini, he wrote:

"The *vali-e-faqih* is empowered to abrogate the religious commitments he has undertaken with the people should he find them contrary to the interests of the nation and Islam. Governing is one dimension of the absolute authority of the *Velayat-e-faqih* and takes precedence over all secondary commandments, even prayer, fasting, and the hajj."[50]

After Khomeini's death in 1989, this authority expanded even more for Ali Khamenei in order to compensate for his significant lack of religious and political stature and charisma.

At the time Khomeini wrote his book, he had no idea that years later a unique confluence of internal and external circumstances would provide an opening for him to insert himself at the center of the 1979 revolution, which at its core was the genuine desire for democracy, popular sovereignty, and economic prosperity, and not so much an Islamic theocratic and autocratic state. But when in power and as the main pillars of *Velayat-e faqih* were established, he and his advisors were well aware of the Achilles heel of their system: that it did not belong in the modern era and was incompatible with true aspirations of the Iranian people. They could sense that from a sociopolitical historical perspective it was already an outdated system. Therefore, the regime, predisposed to defensive governance, views any thoughts, deeds, and position different than its own as a potential existential threat. Its calculus

---

[50] The Islamic Fundamentalism: The New Global Threat, Mohammad Mohaddessin. Seven Locks Press, Washington, DC, 1992, 224 pp

of survival calls for a set of internal and external policies that employs offense as a form of defense. From engineered elections, harsh crackdowns on social and political opposition at home, suppression of women and minorities to sponsorship of terrorism, subversion of regional countries under the pretest of "export of revolution,"[51] to the pursuit of weapons of mass destruction and nuclear arms, the Islamic Republic is on offense against its own people and the world, knowing that the *Velayat-e faqih* system would otherwise fall.

The political structure in Iran is comprised of more unelected bodies than elected bodies. A hybrid of theocracy, autocracy and a touch of electoral process, the structure is designed to provide levers to the Supreme Leader to eliminate any uncooperative and disobedient body, personnel or entity to preserve the system. Thus, leaving no room for free and fair elections in such a regime.[52]

Free and fair elections improve the chances of a peaceful transfer of power. They help to ensure that losing candidates will accept the validity of the election's results, the legitimacy of the ballot box, and cede power to the winner. Not for Iran, though. The most prominent example is the 2009 popular uprising where the world witnessed street killings of the people along with jailing and continued house arrests for the rival candidates. "Nothing that matters is decided by the people in this country," insisted a businessman who participated in the 2009 uprising.[53] Characterizing the Supreme Leader's endorsement of fraudulent election results as opening a "Pandora box," some Iranian analysts say the 2009 election demonstrated "the rift among the ... personalities of the revolution is getting deeper...It is also between

---

[51] http://www.nytimes.com/1981/10/15/world/around-the-world-khomeini-urges-export-of-iranian-revolution.html

[52] Iranian people often refer to the regime as a government from "dark ages" and incapable of catching up with the times.

[53] https://www.theguardian.com/world/2009/jun/14/iran-tehran-election-results-riots

people and their government ... a rift between state and the nation. It is the biggest crisis since the [1979] revolution." [54]

During the 2009 Presidential election, the main dispute was not between genuine reform versus status quo or two fundamentally opposing schools of thought, but was a reflection of deepening crises and the system's failure to either resolve or even contain them. After all, the candidates on both side were vetted and approved by the Guardian Council. Thus, the dispute was merely on tactical differences regarding how best to preserve the *Velayat-e-faqih* system.

Riding on Khomeini's legacy of crushing the opposition during the 1980s, Iran's Supreme Leader, Ali Khamenei, has managed to crush major uprisings in many post-election periods in the late 1990s, in 2003 and 2009. For the 2013 election, his calculations were simply based on zero tolerance for public outbursts even at the cost of his favorite candidate losing to Rouhani. Arguably, it was not Rouhani's popularity that brought him the presidency, rather the deepening internal crises and a weakened state, standing on oppression, that landed him the victory.

The Supreme Leader and His Presidents

Structurally, the office of *vali-e-faqih,* an un-elected body, and the office of president, an elected body, are in perpetual conflict. Former President Hashemi Rafsanjani was the most notable figure among the former presidents vying to replace Ali Khamenei. The two had a long-standing history of deep alliances and deep hostilities. Rafsanjani single handedly elevated Khamenei to status of *vali-e-faqih,* after Ayatollah Khomeini's death in 1989. At the same time, an amendment to Iran's constitution, Articles 57 and 110, was introduced to bring all branches, institutions and

---

[54] https://www.theguardian.com/world/2009/jun/15/iran-elections-protests-mousavi-attacks

organizations of government under the control of the office of *vali-e- faqih*. In exchange, Khamenei abolished the role of the prime minister for the role of presidency endorsing Rafsanjani.[55] A month later, on July 28, 1989, Rafsanjani was elected as a president with 95 percent of the vote. [56]

Public criticism and schism between the two began when Rafsanjani became the richest man in Iran. [57] His second term was filled with major fraud, corruptions coupled with crony capitalism and nepotism. Despised by the Iranian people for his socio-political repressive policies, the regime's insider Rafsanjani was known to support only his own "clan". It is important to note both Mohammad Khatami and Hassan Rouhani gained their political prominence and notoriety during Rafsanjani's two-term presidency. [58]

In August of 1997, on the promise of reform but with the intent of preserving the *vali-e-faqih* system, Khatami became Iran's new president. Rafsanjani quickly seized the leadership of the Expediency Council in order to advise the *vali-e-faqih* on internal disputes between the parliament and the powerful Guardian Council.

---

[55] On June 14, 1989, members of the Majlis and Rafsanjani visited Khamenei to make a covenant with him. In that meeting, Khamenei supported the candidacy of Rafsanjani for president.

[56] http://www.telegraph.co.uk/news/1399838/Ayatollah-Ali-Akbar-Hashemi-Rafsanjani.html

[57] http://www.iranchamber.com/history/arafsanjani/akbar_rafsanjani.php

[58] In different capacity Khatami served as the head of Cultural Ministry during Rafsanjani's term. Rouhani, in similar capacity, was a member of the Supreme Defense Council (1982–1988), member of the High Council for Supporting War and headed its Executive Committee (1986–1988), commander of the Iran Air Defense Force (1986–1991). He was appointed as Deputy to Second-in-Command of Iran's Joint Chiefs of Staff (1988–1989). When Robert C. McFarlane, Reagan' national security adviser, came to Tehran in May 1986, Rouhani was one of the three people who talked to McFarlane about buying weapons. Eventually, this weapons sale became known as the Iran-Contra affair.

In the summer of 1999, Khatami was faced with a major student uprising calling for real reforms while shouting "Down with Dictators." Khatami's rhetoric of "civil society" and "the rule of law" soon became defense of the "constitution based on *Velayat-e-faqih* principle."[59] The tug of war between Khamenei and Rafsanjani became more public and deadly. Increased marginalization of Rafsanjani indirectly manufactured the perception of Khamenei's growing power. High-ranking religious figures, regime insiders and officials began to believe in the shift of power in favor of Khamenei. Taking the side of the "Leader" publicly became a means of survival for many insiders, including Islamic Revolutionary Guards Corps (IRGC) commanders.

In 2005, Rafsanjani, whose political influence was significantly diminished by Khamenei, decided to run for the presidency again. While his public tone with Khamenei was conciliatory, he lost the elections to then-mayor of Tehran, Mahmoud Ahmadinejad, whose message was "for embracing the principles of the revolution."[60]

Four years later, in 2009, Ahmadinejad used Rafsanjani as a laughing stock during his second-term presidential debates characterizing his opponents as "Rafsanjani's puppets." The 2009 disputed elections results led to major uprising and daily protests in more than 50 cities across the nation. Protesters, sensing a slight crack in the suppressive environment, carried a more radical message shouting "Death to Khamenei" and "Government commits the crime and the Leader supports the crime."[61] The disgruntled Rafsanjani stood by and opportunistically refused to condemn the uprising, while Khamenei's pictures were burned, defaced and torn. Khamenei's paranoia became a reality, and he quickly ordered the IRGC to crush the ongoing protests. He also

---

[59] The Myth of Moderation, 1998 (P. 41)

[60] http://www.cnn.com/2005/WORLD/meast/06/18/iran.ballot/

[61] http://www.irannewsnow.com/2009/07/live-blogging-july-30th-iran/

ordered the Minister of Intelligence to investigate Rafsanjani for his role during the unrest. In May of 2013, when Rafsanjani registered his name, again, as a presidential candidate, the ministry concluded he was "actively engaged in the 2009 sedition"[62] to definitively kill any chance of a comeback.

The *vali-e-faqih* did not get along with the "pragmatic" Rafsanjani and "reformer" Khatami. The second term of the "hardline" Ahmadinejad was no exception. On one hand, despite adoptions of several UN Security Council Resolutions against Iran's nuclear program, Ahmadinejad continued to deliver significant expansion for a multi-track nuclear program in line with Khamenei's expectation. On the other, his tumultuous relations with the 'Leader' began with his decision to sack the Intelligence Minister, a Khamenei loyalist. Khamenei overturned Ahmadinejad's decision and the Minister of Intelligence remained in his post. To protest, Ahmadinejad left his office for eleven days. Ahmadinejad began to formulate a power circle with high-ranking IRGC and religious figures, which was immensely threatening to the paranoid *vali-e-faqih*. In return, Khamenei launched a sustained campaign to intimidate Ahmadinejad by arresting his close advisers and accusing him of challenging the *vali-e-faqih* authority.[63]

Rafsanjani, who was actively monitoring their deteriorating relations, decided last-minute to enter the 2013 presidential elections. Khamenei disqualified him and the spotlight was back on their shattered relations once again. [64] In return, Rafsanjani endorsed Hassan Rouhani declaring him as "more suitable" than Khamenei's preferred candidate, the radical Saeed Jalili. [65] In days

[62] http://www.yjc.ir/en/news/981/intelligence-minister-hashemi,-khatami-actively-engaged-in-09-sedition

[63] http://www.alarabiya.net/articles/2012/02/18/195383.html

[64] http://www.theguardian.com/world/2013/may/21/iran-presidential-election-rafsanjani-disqualified

[65] http://www.aljazeera.com/news/middleeast/2013/06/201361116525755648.html

leading up to the 2013 presidential election, Khamenei personally pleaded with the public to fulfill their "duty" and vote, fearing low turnout will be taken as a sign of his diminishing influence domestically and showcase of his weakness internationally.[66] Fearing the repeat of the 2009 uprising, Khamenei settled on Rouhani who mobilized more effectively for a higher turnout than his opponent, Jalili. Thus, the election was wrapped up very quickly and Rouhani was declared the winner with barely over 50 percent of the votes, so that there was not a second-round balloting that would prolong the process at the risk of causing a spark unwittingly to trigger some kind of unrest. [67]

To this date, the Iranian leadership refers to the 2009 post-election uprising as a clear warning. Ahmad Janati, head of the Assembly of Experts, claims "Seditionists in 2009 (uprising) pulled the country into a long chaos and anarchy such that it requires years to compensate for the damage to the system. They were thinking about the overthrow of the Islamic Republic, which means the issue was not the elections or something like that at all but to overthrow the Islamic Republic and Islamic Revolution and replace it with a secular government. If this sedition (uprising) had succeeded, this system would have been suppressed (defeated) completely and the Islamic regime would have been dismantled."[68]

---

[66] http://www.rferl.org/content/iran-election-president-/24975986.html

[67] https://www.foreignaffairs.com/articles/iran/2013-06-16/why-rouhani-won-and-why-khamenei-let-him?page=show

[68] http://www.ncr-iran.org/en/news/iran-protests/21821-iran-regime-officials-terrified-warnings-about-a-repeat-of-2009-uprising

Source: 2016 Official website of the President of the Islamic Republic of Iran

For his part, Rafsanjani, Rouhani's longtime mentor, declared the election results as his greatest accomplishment, and a new phase of furious and potentially fatal showdown between Khamenei and Rafsanjani began.[69]

Rouhani and the Upcoming Election

President Rouhani's claim of sweeping victory through promises of a better economy and friendlier relations with the international community in 2013 began with the push to reach an agreement with the world's powers dubbed as the Joint Comprehensive Plan of Action (JCPOA). In the summer of 2015, the agreement was finally reached and the implementation began in 2016. Iran's Supreme Leader endorsed the agreement in October 2015 with tacit warning toward the United States that despite the landmark agreement, Iran would continue to view America as the

---

[69] http://www.defenddemocracy.org/media-hit/the-new-rouhani/#sthash.gd5x3m00.dpuf

"Great Satan," possibly to appease "hard-liners," some of whom wept openly after Parliament voted to endorse the deal.[70]

Iran's crippling economy due to international sanctions was one of the main drivers that brought the Supreme Leader and the President to agree on the nuclear deal. Yet, both elected and un-elected bodies have criticized Rouhani for his failure to deliver on his promises.   On August 1, 2016, Khamenei publicly criticized Rouhani by saying "Was it not agreed that the unjust sanctions be lifted to have [positive] effects on people's lives? Is any tangible impact seen on people's lives after six months?"[71] Members of Iran's parliament called on Rouhani to "explain to the people why sanctions and threats have not been removed and are becoming more intense every day." Key players in IRGC's circles are saying "None of the big European banks will work with us. They have zero dealings with us. At the moment, no dollar transactions are being conducted with Iran, and this has created problems in all of our business dealings."

All factions, including the President, are fearing the growing movement of labor strikes and protests. In February 2017, more than 200 labor protests in 47 cities and towns called for benefits and their backed wages.[72]   A month later, more than nine cities faced major demonstrations with crowds shouting "Students, workers, teachers, nurses, unity, unity." [73]

By all accounts, Rouhani can potentially become Iran's first one-term president. Nevertheless, the internal dispute is driven from an existential crisis, with each faction arguing that the other's

---

[70] https://www.nytimes.com/2015/10/22/world/middleeast/iran-nuclear-deal-ayatollah-ali-khamenei.html?_r=0

[71] http://www.al-monitor.com/pulse/originals/2016/09/iran-president-rouhani-reelection-second-term-ahmadinejad.html

[72] http://ncr-iran.org/en/news/iran-protests/22325-a-round-up-of-february-2017-protests

[73] http://ncr-iran.org/en/ncri-statements/iran-protests/22353-iran-thousands-of-retirees-protest-across-the-country

approach will lead to the overthrow of the regime. The Rafsanjani-Rouhani faction demand their share of power and some tactical maneuvering to preserve the regime's survival, while Khamenei repeatedly warns that the domino effect of any opening to the outside world, and, more importantly, any domestic opening will lead to the end of the Islamic Republic. The irony is that both outlooks are correct and consistent with the worsening overall status of the system.

More crippling than any time before, this is the paradox and dilemma that the regime is facing in the 2017 elections: It cannot preserve itself by maintaining the status quo, while it cannot survive a transformational change either. Such calculation still stands for the upcoming elections in Iran. Yet, Rafsanjani is now dead.

Rafsanjani's Death and What Lies Ahead

On January 8, 2017, the world learned about the sudden death of Ali Akbar Hashemi Rafsanjani. The New York Times described his death as "political factions knew immediately that any space by reformers to maneuver had just significantly decreased."[74]

As two of the original officers of the *Velayat-e faqih* operation from the outset of Ayatollah Khomeini's tenure, Ali Khamenei and Hashemi Rafsanjani understood, as few others did, the dynamic nature of the revolutionary enterprise. Both recognized that an Islamic republic that structurally lacked popular sovereignty would not long survive without continually demanding respect and pursuing influence externally while requiring sacrifice and enforcing subservience internally. It is for this reason that the *Velayat-e faqih* office maintains a focus on image-building propaganda for the leader of the revolution, ever promoting the

---

[74] https://www.nytimes.com/2017/01/08/world/middleeast/iran-ali-akbar-hashemi-rafsanjani-dies.html

stature of its "heroic" godfather, Ayatollah Khomeini. Propaganda is used to rally and unify the IRGC, mobilize the paramilitary forces such as the Bassijis for public crackdowns, and organize the religious sector across the nation for Friday prayers in accordance with prescribed policy themes. [75]

Many speculate with Rafsanjani out of the picture, the aging Khamenei will move toward more consolidation of power in favor of the Islamic Revolutionary Guard Corp (IRGC) to seal his legacy in the upcoming presidential elections in May as the issue of Khamenei's succession also heavily looms in the air.

Rouhani seems to fear that history will repeat itself and he will experience Rafsanjani's fate in the upcoming elections. One can argue Khamenei's calculus is from the position of power. On the contrary, over the years his power has eroded and his circle of trust is shrinking. While many have moved seamlessly between so-called reformist and hardliner patronage, the driving motive seems less to be ideology than competition for resources and leverage. Even the staunch supporters of *Velayat-e faqih*, such as the three Larijani brothers, who rose to positions of influence within the Parliament, Guardian Council, judiciary, broadcasting (IRIB) and Foreign Ministry, are viewed with suspicion by Khamenei for this very reason.[76]

Ali Khamenei has survived by surrounding himself with a small and shrinking circle of trusted advisors, including his own son Mojtaba, who leads the Bassijis and oversees all his financial affairs operating beyond the reach of sanctions. Some have speculated that Mojtaba is being groomed to become his father's successor. As much as regime figures may jostle for primacy and influence over Iranian policy, all are charter members of an enterprise whose overriding mission is their collective survival in

---

[75] http://nationalinterest.org/feature/what-washington-doesnt-get-about-iran-16411

[76] http://www.pbs.org/wgbh/pages/frontline/tehranbureau/2009/08/nepotism-the-larijani-dynasty.html

power. What recent trends reveal is that the Supreme Leader's diminishing power is accompanied by, and likely further eroded by, the more open rivalries at play in the upcoming elections.

With Rafsanjani out of the picture, the revolutionary enterprise will run on an unleashed, varied and unmanaged push for reformists and hardliners around Khamenei. The Iranian President, Hassan Rouhani, will have to navigate much rougher waters to maintain the reformists' base and his loyalty to Khamenei, all at the same time. For his part, Khamenei faces the same dilemma in managing the hardliners, whom may feel emboldened and want to push for further consolidation of power in their favor. Either way, in the 2017 elections, both Rouhani and Khamenei are facing a much higher risk and threat in comparison to four years ago.

It is within this context that Iran's behavior over the last 12 months can be understood and analyzed. The stakes are higher for the Islamic Republic of Iran; hence, the machinery of killing at home is hard at work. In the last 12 months, according to the UN Human Rights Monitor, Iran ranks first in the world when it comes to the number of executions per capita. As denounced by Human Rights Watch, Tehran's mass executions of Sunnis that took place in 2016 are a "shameful low point in its human rights record." During Rouhani's presidency, nearly 3,000 people have been executed.[77]

Iran's terror at home is matched by its terror abroad and expansionist efforts in the region. In 2016, a high record of IRGC fighters and commanders were killed on Syrian and Iraqi soil because of their extraterritorial operations and foreign military missions. According to U.S. Intelligence, the number of active members of the extra-territorial branch of the IRGC, the Quds

---

[77]http://www.iranfocus.com/en/index.php?option=com_content&view=article&id=3080 9:iran-under-rouhani-s-rule-nearly-3-000-people-have-been-executed&catid=4:iran-general&Itemid=109

Force, in Iraq and Syria are in the tens of thousands. Supporting Assad's army against the Syrian opposition is in fact in line with Iran's expansionist and fundamentalist vision for the region. In the summer of 2016, in Syria alone, there were 70,000 Iranian regime proxy forces.[78]

Based on a recent and extensive studies by two distinguished European NGOs, the European Iraqi Freedom Association and The International Committee In Search of Justice, the IRGC has been meddling in the affairs of all 14 Muslim countries in the region. It is directly involved in the hidden occupation of four countries in particular: Iraq, Syria, Yemen and Lebanon. In all four, the IRGC has a direct and considerable military presence. The same study reveals that IRGC has set up terrorist affiliates or networks in at least 12 regional countries and has carried out terrorist activities in 13 out of the 14 countries.

On the nuclear front, according to the latest report by IAEA, Iran is not complying with the terms of the nuclear agreement. Last November, Iran violated the terms of the deal for the second time since 2015, exceeding a limit of 130 metric tons for heavy water. At the time, the State Department acknowledged "that Iran made no effort to hide this, hide what it was doing from the IAEA." [79]

More recently, Iran has engaged in Ballistic Missile tests, which defies the spirit of UN Security Council Resolution 1929, passed in 2010, and UN Resolution 2231, passed in 2015, where the Security Council endorsed the nuclear deal. In recent days, Iran's behavior in the Persian Gulf, harassing the USS Invincible on two occasions

---

[78] http://isjcommittee.com/2017/03/isj-eifa-report-destructive-role-irans-islamic-revolutionary-guard-corps-irgc-middle-east/

[79] http://www.foxnews.com/world/2016/11/10/iran-violates-limit-established-in-nuclear-deal-un-finds.html

in the Strait of Hormuz, is all part of the regime's egregious record.[80]

The IRGC has an intelligence unit that functions in parallel to the Ministry of Intelligence (MOIS) when it comes to coordinating terror at home and abroad. Both of these entities are under the supervision of the Iran's Supreme Leader, who is fully aware what may lie ahead, hence the aggressive drive for influence externally while elevating oppression at home.

The "Moderate" Fallacy

If one were to poll political experts on how they view various political factions and measure reform in Iran, a consensus would likely be elusive. Ending the loyalty screening and disqualification by the Guardian Council of candidates for office would be an obvious metric, as would measures to end violation of the rights and sponsorship of terrorism and subversive and destabilizing activities. Yet, sadly enough, many in the West portray elections in Iran as a contest between hard-liners, reformers and moderates where, in fact, none exist. Some, wittingly or not, have lowered the bar so much that figures, such as Hashemi Rafsanjani, Mohammad Khatami, and Hassan Rouhani, who have a horrific record of human rights violations, suppression and assassination of dissidents at home and abroad, sponsorship of terrorism, and advancing of Iran's nuclear weapons program are praised as "reformist" and 'Moderate."

In 1987, in the aftermath of the Irangate debacle, a Washington Post editorial titled "The 'Moderate' Fantasy" stated "The fundamental trouble with the concept of moderation in and of itself as a virtue is that it is relative and derivative. A thug can get to be a 'moderate' merely by indicating cryptically with a few

---

[80] http://www.npr.org/sections/parallels/2017/02/03/513229839/did-irans-ballistic-missile-test-violate-a-u-n-resolution

ambiguous gestures that he is somewhat better than the butcher he works for or somewhat less maniacal or malevolent that he used to be or than his best buddies still are. Accordingly, by being only slightly to the west of a monster, he can gain 'moderate' status." In 2016, Wendy Sherman, the Obama administration's chief American nuclear negotiator had noted that "There are hardliners in Iran, and then there are hard-hardliners in Iran." [81]

In the 2017 elections, no matter how hard Iran's media and its overseas echo chambers try to portray the election as a meaningful choice between "hard-line" and "reformist" factions, the true narrative of the election will be about which one of the servants of the *Velayat-e faqih* system and what sort of factional equilibrium will be selected by the *Vali-e faqih* as the least detrimental to the survival of the regime in the very rocky path ahead.

Three Components of Khamenei's Election Calculus

The central point in analysis of the presidential elections in Iran is the understanding of the components of Supreme Leader Ali Khamenei's calculus when crafting his approach.

1- The election must not serve as an impetus or trigger for a popular revolt against the system. That is a red line. As explained earlier, the enduring effect of the 2009 uprisings heavily weighed on the 2013 election when Khamenei, unlike during the 2005 and 2009 elections, refrained from using his tremendous resources to engineer the elections in the final days.

In 2017, similar to 2013, the first and foremost component of Khamenei's calculus is to prevent a repeat of the 2009 popular unrest at any cost and by any means. In short, that's his red line, which must not be crossed by any strategy, plans or deeds of his faction and the IRGC for the sake of wining. Rival factions will no

[81] https://www.usnews.com/opinion/articles/2016-05-03/calling-hassan-khomeini-and-other-iranians-moderates-is-a-misnomer

doubt be made to understand that they need to adhere to this red line. In this context, it is hard to imagine that he would have the Guardian Council to reject Rouhani's candidacy or publicly oppose him – something that Khamenei did not hesitate to do when Ahmadinejad sought his approval earlier this year. With the death of Rafsanjani, Rouhani has lost an irreplaceable ally given his nature as a survivor in the course of almost four decades of factional infightings and constant change of alliances. It could very well be possible that Rouhani would move closer to Khamenei as a political cover as he seeks a second term, making it easier for Khamenei to tolerate a much weaker Rouhani.

2- America's new administration. Since 1979, the Islamic Republic has experienced dealing with both Republican and Democratic administrations, and the general feeling in Tehran has been that they have a fairly reliable playbook on how to deal with a new administration regardless of its party affiliation. The 2017 election, however, posed a new challenge for the regime. First and foremost, the "Golden era" of former President Barack Obama, as described in Tehran, is over.[82] Then-candidate Donald Trump's tough rhetoric was viewed as mere campaign bombast by a figure who ultimately is a deal maker and if the price is right, is willing to make a deal. However, since Trump's inauguration, the words and deeds of the new administration and the makeup of its national security team have totally upended this perspective and seem to have immensely unsettled Tehran, introducing a significant level of policy paralysis. The *New York Times* reported from Tehran that "there is little doubt that the clerics have been thrown off balance. One analyst with access to government deliberations said that hard-liners in Iran were confused and did not know how to deal with the situation. Some in the establishment are opting for the

---

[82] http://origin-nyi.thehill.com/blogs/pundits-blog/the-administration/307245-donald-trumps-iran-policy-can-finally-correct-for-obama

same rhetoric and tactics they used under Mr. Obama, but in reality, this is uncharted territory, he said."[83] This anxiety is best displayed by the uncharacteristic silence of Supreme Leader Ali Khamenei, so far, in the flurry of statements and actions from the new administration and Tehran's erratic responses. This new dimension will be significant as Tehran struggles to draw a new playbook for dealing with the new administration, particularly as Khamenei and his circle of trusted advisors are working hard to strategize for the upcoming elections. The same *New York Times* article states "Hard-liners are deeply critical of Mr. Rouhani and are increasingly dismissing him as a figure of the past, the right answer in the Obama era but the wrong one now. Hamidreza Taraghi, a hard-liner analyst, told the Times "Mr. Rouhani speaks beautiful words, but they are empty. We can deal with Mr. Trump. He is a businessman, but we should not compromise." There are others who argue that by keeping Rouhani around, Khamenei could continue on his own agenda while benefiting from the false image of Rouhani as a "reformist" perpetuated by the pro-engagement advocates in the West particularly as the new U.S. administration is putting its Iran policy together.

3- Khamenei's health and the issue of succession. Khamenei suffers from Prostate cancer and has been under treatment since 2014. French daily, *Le Figaro*, reported in 2015 that according to doctors the cancer had spread extensively and Khamenei may not survive it.[84] Whatever the extent of his cancer, it is obvious that Khamenei's health is declining and the issue of his succession, although a major taboo to be discussed publicly, is being intensely talked about within the inner circles. A committee to consider possible candidates for the post of Supreme Leader is understood to have been established by the Assembly of Experts and a list of

---

[83] https://www.nytimes.com/2017/02/03/world/middleeast/iran-trump.html

[84] http://www.rudaw.net/english/middleeast/iran/01032015

several candidates is reported to have been circulated internally. By all indication, Khamenei intends to resolve the issue of succession before he dies.[85] Given the highly fractious nature of his regime's factions in comparison to 1989, when his predecessor Ayatollah Khomeini died, Khamenei fears if the issue is not resolved while he is still alive, the next Supreme leader could end up being someone outside of his trusted circle, cutting their hands from power and wealth. He desires Ebrahim Raisi, a 56-year-old conservative cleric who is in charge of Astan Quds Razavi, the wealthiest charity in the Muslim world, and with immense political clout within Iran's theocracy, to be his successor. [86] However, in Khamenei's fast shrinking circle of trusted figures, Raisi also happens to be his favored figure for the presidential contest, someone whom Khamenei believes can rally all of his loyal factions. And there lies a huge dilemma for Khamenei. Although there is no legal or constitutional barrier for a president in Iran to become the supreme leader later, as was the case with Khamenei himself in 1989, Raisi's candidacy, however, could be a double-edged sword. He was "a member of the infamous 'Death Committee,' a four-man special judicial panel that ordered the executions of thousands of political prisoners in the summer of 1988. Running in Iran's presidential election would expose Raisi to embarrassing questions about his role in the massacre."[87] Therefore, if Raisi enters the presidential race and is defeated, then his chances as Khamenei's successor would also diminish immensely. And if Khamenei were to "engineer" Raisi's victory, then he would risk triggering a popular revolt, something Khamenei wants to avoid at any cost.

---

[85] http://www.huffingtonpost.com/ali-hashem/khameneis-plan-for-succes_b_12599372.html

[86] https://www.washingtonpost.com/opinions/global-opinions/irans-likely-next-supreme-leader-is-no-friend-of-the-west/2016/09/26/eb3becc0-79fb-11e6-bd86-b7bbd53d2b5d_story.html?utm_term=.d878cce8f027

[87] https://www.iranhumanrights.org/2017/03/ebrahim-raeisi-presidential-election/

Given the speed and weight of domestic and regional developments and as Washington drafts its new Iran policy, one can understand why Khamenei would prefer to wait until the very last minute to reveal his plans for the 2017 election.

Conclusion

The 2017 election could well prove to be a very consequential chapter in the history of the Islamic Republic. The confluence of several detrimental forces, the Iranian people's hunger for democratic transformation and their despise for the *Velayat-e faqih* regime, the falling political and ideological prowess of Supreme Leader Khamenei as the chief wielder of power in the Islamic Republic, the ever-growing factional infighting, the death of Rafsanjani, a main pillar of the regime and its last king-maker, a more compromised and fading Rouhani, and the prospect for a new U.S. policy to counter Tehran's external transgressions and block its geo-strategic breathing channels, could expose the regime's strategic vulnerabilities. Therefore, regardless of outcome, the post-election path of this regime will not be toward reform or moderation, but a deepening crisis of legitimacy and survival.

Equally important, is the understanding that the future of Iran lies with its people who aspire democracy, human rights, and peaceful co-existence within themselves and the outside world. Four years ago, and in the aftermath of Rouhani's presidential win, John Hanna of the Foundation for Defense of Democracies wrote, "the election once again exposed the ever-widening chasm that exists between the Iranian people and the Islamic Republic. That is truly the big strategic revelation that the United States should take away... It's not hard at all to imagine that were they ever given a genuinely free choice to rid themselves lock, stock, and barrel of Ruhollah Khomeini's destructive experiment in theocratic tyranny, the Iranian people would jump on it. Khamenei and the Revolutionary Guard have worked tirelessly the past four years to crush that popular yearning for change... Against all odds, the wellspring of hope for democratic transformation and the desire to escape the outlaw status, shame, and isolation inflicted on their great nation by an increasingly despotic regime remains alive and well in the Iranian people."[88]

Any other reading of the 2017 elections would lead, as before, to the endless cycle of hope and disappointment for the policymaker.

Dr. Ramesh Sepehrrad is a scholar practitioner at the School of Conflict Analysis and Resolution (SCAR) at George Mason University, Fairfax, Virginia, USA. Dr. Sepehrrad has focused her research and field work on Iranian affairs as it relates to human rights, gender equality and U.S. policy. From 1992-2015, Dr. Sepehrrad served as conference director, moderator and panelist at various academic institutions, congressional seminars and United Nations events in North America, Europe, Asia and Latin America.

Reza Bulorchi is an Iran policy analyst based in Washington, DC. He has been published in various outlets such the Wall Street Journal, the Washington Post, the Washington Times, The National Interest, and the Asia Times, among others.

---

[88] http://www.defenddemocracy.org/media-hit/iranian-election-reflections-part-3/

The roots of the Iranian terror threat

Walid Phares

The mere description of the Iranian regime's aggressive policies in the Middle East over the past few years, its growing and undeterred nuclear ambitions, and its backing of several terror networks across the Levant and Arabia compel us to reexamine the historical and philosophical roots of this terror, visible since the inception of the Iranian Islamic Republic in 1979. The 21st century saw a catastrophic expansion of the Iranian Khomeinist power across the Middle East and the Red Sea and an unleashing of its destructive forces across the region, but these realities have their genesis in the 20th century, a previous era which directed their path and rise over the last three decades. It is thus important for the public—and for researchers—to reexamine the stages through which the so-called "Islamic Republic," a sister of Daesh's "Islamic State," came to exist, how it evolved and survived the passage from the Cold War into the post 9/11 era, and how the Republic increased in power despite internal revolts and rebellions, peaking with the Green Revolution of June 2009. How the Ayatollah's power came to exist and eliminate its opponents is only the *original* question. How it has been able to terrorize the international community from Beirut to Buenos Aires with impunity is another, greater question.

For over 35 years, much academic research, many books, and numerous articles have been published on Iran's revolution and its Islamic ideology. Aside from the literature produced by the Iranian opposition, most of the narrative on Iran's regime has been somewhat affected by apologists for that regime. Though a significant number of publications in Europe, the United States, and the rest of the world have been able to escape that influence and offer readers a comprehensive history of the Iranian regime and its mutation into a regional threat, one should notice that until the last few years, the core of academic research, particularly in high education institutions and prominent think tanks on both sides of the Atlantic, have been sympathetic to the Tehran elite and its narrative. The central arguments made by the apologist academics are:

(1) The revolution was led by the Islamist clergy, the most legitimate social and spiritual force in the eyes of a majority of Iranians, then;

(2) Once the Shah was toppled, the Ayatollahs protected their revolution by eliminating all other secular revolutionary forces;

(3) The new regime, legitimized by a popular referendum on an Islamist constitution, has been representing the people of Iran—or at least the overwhelming majority—while inspiring other peoples in the region to struggle for their identity and against colonialism.

These premises were advanced as a creed to understand Iranian policies domestically and internationally. The center of this creed—despite all terror acts and activities over the decades—insisted on the original legitimacy of this regime, on its popular acceptance, and thus on the need to eventually settle any problems with the ruling regime, not with an alternative opposition.

The explanation for this easy availability of apologist material in two crucial realms, academia and the media, resides in the fact that the Tehran regime had the lobbying capabilities, both financial and political, necessary to sustain this intellectual legitimization process for decades. Put simply, from the time the Ayatollahs were able to seize power in Tehran, the regime shrewdly invested its Petrodollars in the nerve center of the Western intellectual elite to defend the regime and push back against its critics. The Iranian regime and its parallel in the Sunni world—the Muslim Brotherhood—were the two Middle East-based forces most successful in impacting the West with their narrative in a such a sustained manner as to produce a defensive shield that has allowed the political and moral survival of suppressive forces.

While many historical accounts have already been published about the details of the early stage of the Iranian popular revolution against the Shah regime, of the Ayatollah Khomeini's coup against his allies in the first revolution, and the long and painful repression that then took place inside Iran, many in the international community, particularly within the classrooms, have been unable to capture and articulate the reality of the Iranian regime. For example, propaganda efforts by the regime itself and its allies have spent significant efforts to link the final product of the 1979 revolution to the botched revolution of Mosaddeq in the 1950s. But the historical reality is otherwise: The change that struck Iran in 1979 was double, almost identical to the first two layers of the Arab Spring in 2011. There was a deep wave of discontent coming from the depth of civil society, which was the actual force that toppled the Shah, but the civil society force was immediately followed by an Islamist force that toppled the first wave, eliminated its secular and liberal leadership, and instead installed a fascist-like regime. Without understanding the two-wave equation of the late 1970s, it would be difficult to understand the relationship between the regime and the Iranian people over the following decades and—more importantly—the present state of affairs in Iran, particularly since the Green revolution in 2009.

Significance of Syria in the Genesis of Terror

In June of 1976, during the second year of the conflict in Lebanon, Syria's president, Dictator Hafez Assad, ordered his troops to invade his neighbor country, starting with the Bekaa. One year after the invasion, which was supposed to end the war, clashes erupted with the local resistance movement, and another generalized conflict exploded in 1978 between the occupying army led by the Alawite regime in Damascus, their local Lebanese allies, and pro-Baathist Palestinian factions against a coalition of militias called the Lebanese Forces and some brigades of the Lebanese regular army who refused to follow orders from Damascus. The Syrians lost some areas they had occupied in 1976 to the Lebanese resistance but continued to retain most of the country. Assad had secured many areas in Lebanon and had subdued the PLO, but he was still very much isolated in the mostly Sunni Arab world. He was surrounded by a Sunni dominated Iraq, a NATO member Turkey, a pro-Western Jordan, and a U.S. allied Israel. His control of large swaths of territories in Lebanon was his only expansion outside Syria. The Alawi dominated Baathist regime in Damascus had no future in the region, but for a major change that took place in Iran that year: the fall of the Shah.

The 1979 Revolution

Initially, the Iranian revolution was a popular uprising against the Shah dictatorship and for freedom and democracy. The monarchy in Iran under the Pahlavi dynasty was certainly pro-Western and assisted the United States in its containment of the Soviet Union and communism. It also played a role in the balance of power between Israel and the Arab countries during the several wars, as Iraq and the Gulf states were locked in tensions with Tehran. But the Shah's policies in the realm of domestic affairs pitted the regime against large segments of society, particularly the leftwing, labor, students, and liberal factions. Despite many reforming measures, a political movement was building against the regime. But the opposition, though partially leftist with the Communists playing a central role, was much wider than the progressive circles. On the other side of the spectrum, a majority of the Shia clergy was traditionally siding with the Shah's power and profiting from his protection. The upper class of clerics also possessed quite a bit of property as one of the largest landowners in the country.

When the education of women and the agrarian reforms were considered and pushed by the government, the clergy felt threatened in its own backyard. For poor people to obtain lands, it indicated a high likelihood that the clerics would lose some. The empowerment of Iranian women was also a menacing factor to the religious circles, particularly those fundamentalists. Gradually, many religious leaders, not all, shifted to the side of the opposition. Leading the hardliners among the clerics was Ayatollah Ruhallah Khomeini, who had been exiled from the country for his radicalization of clerics. Exiled Khomeini went to Iraq, where he agitated the Shia against the secular Baath regime. He was then banned from Iraq and went to France where he prepared for the takeover of Tehran.

Khomeini was backed by a hardcore of radical Mullahs inside Iran's clerical institutions. He belonged to the extremist brand of Shia Jihadism opposite to the more mainstream brand of "Shia quietists" backed by some Ayatollahs in Iran and symbolized by Grand Ayatollah Sistani in Iraq. In addition, Shia Jihadis were also influenced by a messianic vision of end of times advanced by some scholars about a theological announcement of the return of the vanished Imam. Khomeini stirred the Jihadi Shia movement to become the core of his force and harangued most clerics to back his demand for a removal of the Shah. He thus appeared as a spiritual father to the vast opposition to the Shah. Khomeini skillfully placed himself as a Patriarch of the people uninterested in power. The reality, however, was that he was preparing for the power grab of the century, including the launching of a radical Islamic regime, which would inspire Jihadists of all backgrounds, Shia and Sunnis alike.

Claiming he was leading the opposition to the systematic suppression, execution and imprisonments of leaders and members of democratic forces by the Shah's secret police, due to the lack of democratic institutions in Iran, Khomeini used its network of mullahs to gradually grab the leadership of the revolution. The forces of the opposition ranged from conservatives to religious, from centrists and youth activists to the traditional leftwing and the far left. The initial revolution was not Islamist, let alone Jihadist. It was a popular uprising seeking massive reforms and free elections. Some had even proposed a constitutional monarchy to replace the Shah's absolute monarchy. But in the center of the growing and expanding movement, Khomeini was carefully pushing for a regime change while working on eliminating his associates in the revolution. In short, he hijacked the leadership of the revolution as it was progressing.

The process was complex, but its end product simple. The Khomeinists, like the Bolsheviks in 1917 Russia and the Muslim Brotherhood in 2011 Egypt, were the radicals who seized power, not just from the Shah but truly from their own allies, and installed a fascist republic, setting the clock back from a pro-Western but authoritarian monarchy to an Islamist-Jihadist-fundamentalist regime, widening the oppression from political suppression to that of a totalitarian iron fist.

As soon as the Shah abdicated, the Khomeinist elite insured rapid control of the armed forces, which were counted among the best and most powerful of the region. Western educated and trained high ranking officers of the army and police were exiled, tortured, jailed or executed—not only those who were accused of atrocities against civilians and political activists, but all those who opposed the Islamist ideology imposed by Khomeini.

After gutting the Army, the Islamists turned against the liberals and the progressives who had helped them in the revolution against the previous regime. Socialists and democrats, who were at the forefront of the struggle for a political change and without whom the Ayatollahs would not have been able to obtain Western sympathies, were the first to be destroyed. Unions, foundations, NGOs and other civil society groups were dismantled and replaced with loyal Khomeinist entities.

Shortly after the revolution, a powerful national militia called the Revolutionary Guards, or Sepah Pasdaran, was established to "defend the regime against its enemies." This was the equivalent of the Hitlerian SS or the Soviet KGB, an agency of oppression whose aim was to eliminate any opposition to the clerical regime. The Pasdaran were backed by the Basij, a sub militia of neighborhood forces tasked with close spying and suppression against dissidents in urban areas. Soon enough, the Ayatollah's regime would turn against what was a powerful and organized partner in the revolution, the Mujahidin Khalq (MEK), a major player of the initial revolt.

Iraq-Iran war

During September of 1980, Iraq invaded the southwestern region of Iran. Saddam's armies, well equipped by the Soviets but also with sophisticated French and British weapons, thrust through the borders with Iran and headed toward the ethnic Arab area of Iran, known as Khuzestan or Ahwaz. Some call it Arabstan. The area stretches from east of Basra, south along the Persian Gulf. Iraq's Baathist regime seemed to have conducted a unilateral offensive to gain territory and power. While it may have been part of the grand design of Pan Arabism to reunify all Arabs into one Pan Arab state, this may have not been the primary reason for the military expedition into Iran. Iraq and Iran, despite long standing enmity and clashes across the borders, had signed an agreement in 1975, known as Shat al Arab accord, moderated by the Arab League. Shah Mohammad Reza Pahlavi and the Iraqi government agreed to freeze their disagreements and demarcated the borders, particularly in the south. Both sides, though authoritarian inside their countries, knew that a direct invasion of the other side would generate a useless and endless war. Why did Saddam Hussein, whose real competitor was Hafez Assad in Syria and with whom he had been engaged in a Mukhabarat war for years, turn his attention east and unleash a suicidal blitzkrieg into Iran?

What triggered the Iraqi dictator's campaign into his neighbor was the new Iranian campaign to extend the Ayatollah's regime into Iraq's central and southern provinces. Khomeini called for an Islamic revolution in Iraq and an overthrow of Baghdad's government. The new Islamist regime in Iran began—from its inception—to mobilize for an uprising in Iraq. A Khomeinist Jihad—read a Shia Jihad—was underway against the mostly Sunni regime of Baghdad, parallel to the Sunni Jihad underway in Afghanistan against the Soviets. Khomeini declared its religious war against the Istikbar, or the imperialist designs of both Russia and the United States. Saddam happened to be the shield of the Sunnis in a conflict Khomeini was transforming into a Shia-Sunni clash. Another reason for Iraq's campaign into Iran was Saddam's perception that Iraq was now sandwiched between two bellicose powers, Iran and Syria. Tehran was calling for an Islamist uprising against Iraq's government, and Assad was calling for a Baathist coup against his competitor. It was one dictator against two, and Saddam hit first. Saddam projected that all Arab Sunnis would come to his help against the radical Shia regime in Tehran. He imagined that both the Soviets and the United States, though locked in a Cold War, had common interest in containing Iran's new regime. Beyond these international considerations, Saddam hoped that Iran's ethnic Arabs would acclaim him and join his forces. The main reason for Iraq's failed campaign was simply that the Iranian people were unable to rise against the Khomeinist regime.

Using the war to crush the internal opposition

Once engaged in the full-fledged war with the Iraqi armed forces, Iran's regime used the military confrontation with an outside foe to crush its internal opposition. In the months following the toppling of the Shah regime, many forces within the ranks of the revolution, particularly the Mujahidin Khalq, opposed the transformation of the country into a fundamentalist religious regime. Khomeini could not easily destroy his secular and progressive opposition without mobilizing Iranian masses to support him in a war against an outside enemy with domestic allies. When hostilities began, the MEK and most Iranian political forces were clearly siding with the Iranian state against the invasion. They were accused of internal violence by the regime. The real reason behind Khomeini's suppression of the MEK's political activists was nothing apart from seizing the regime entirely and launching his ideological project of an Islamic Republic, a first step toward the creation of a regional—then world—Imamate, a Shia version of the Sunni Caliphate. Step one was to bring down the monarch, which necessitated working with secularists and liberals. Once the Shah was out of the way, however, Khomeini's Islamists directed their pressure on the armed forces, even though they had abandoned the Shah during the revolution. Once the military was marginalized and a parallel force was established as militias of the regime (the Pasdaran and Basij), the remaining political forces that marched against the Shah became targets. Repeating the Bolshevik model of the early 1920s, the Jihadi Ayatollahs of Iran eliminated their comrades in the revolution slice by slice. The clerics close to Khomeini marginalized any religious figures in Qom and Teheran who did not see eye to eye with them on state policies and ideologies.

But the most stalwart obstruction against the Islamists seizing the entire state was the organized militants of the MEK. Tilting to the progressive left but attached to the Muslim identity of the Iranian people, whom they were planning on transforming into a

103

modern day identity, MEK appeared as the only credible force that could stop Khomeini from building his Jihadi republic. Now that the Shah's influence was winding down and the armed forces were subordinated to the Pasdaran (as the German Army was subdued by the SS during WWII), and as the fervor of a patriotic war exploded against Iraq's invasion, Khomeini struck against his last rival: the Mujahidin Khalq.

The movement had been organizing rallies across the country to oppose the erection of a pure religious state. On June 20, 1981, the turning point occurred: the 500,000 participant non-violent demonstration led by the MEK in Tehran was attacked by the Revolutionary Guards. Khomeini had ordered the IRGC and other militias to open fire on the demonstrators. Tehran's radio, repeatedly, announced Khomeini's order on air. Dozens were killed and hundreds arrested. With the elimination of the MEK as a political force, Khomeini tightened control of media, radio, television, and suppressed political life and pluralism. As the dust of war was blurring the vision of the international community and most Iranians were drawn to back their government against the Iraqis, the Ayatollahs systematically destroyed the fabric of pluralism in Iran. The educational system was transformed into a propaganda machine endorsing the regime's doctrines; women's rights were dramatically reduced; political freedoms were eliminated; and ethnic minorities were further oppressed— particularly the Kurds, Arabs, and Baluchis.

As Khomeini was sending tens of thousands of civilian recruits, including children, to be massacred in a war against the Iraqi army while keeping his best forces of the Pasdaran to defend the regime on the inside, the Ayatollahs managed to eliminate their opposition, establish a dictatorship, and prepare their new regime to expand beyond its borders once their war with Saddam was over.

It was during that same war, from 1980 to 1988, that Tehran's Islamist regime crushed a Kurdish autonomy movement centered in Mahabad, suppressed an Arab movement in Ahwaz, and pushed back against the Baluchis in the East of the country. The war with Iraq, though the latter was first to invade, was intentionally stretched by Khomeini to the longest possible conflict in order to ensure a systematic elimination of any opposition to his designs. Any criticism to Khomeini and his Islamic republic resulted in an accusation of collaboration with the enemy during a time of war. The punishment was jailing, torture, and execution. Thousands of Iranians fled the country into exile. A real *Republic of Fear* was installed, and Iranian oil revenues were seized by the cartel of religious leaders, which allowed them to fund their platform at will.

The US embassy's hostage crisis

To create immediate cementing around the regime, Khomeinist partisans unleashed what became known as the U.S. hostage crisis starting in 1979. Hundreds of militant supporters of the new Islamic regime stormed the U.S. embassy in Tehran and captured dozens of diplomats and employees and kept them detained for many weeks and months. Many wondered why the Islamic regime would engage from day one in a confrontation with the United States via terror methods. A thorough historical analysis reconstructing the events of the early days of the revolution concludes that Khomeini needed a primary enemy to gather the people against, and that was the United States. America was backing the Sunni Islamists in the region, such as Saudi Arabia, the Muslim Brotherhood and to a certain extent Pakistan. Moreover, the U.S. was also backing the Sunni Mujahidin in Afghanistan. Khomeini feared the U.S. would eventually back the Salafi Jihadists against the Shia regime in Iran. Hence, seizing diplomats and deterring the U.S. government was designed to establish a balance of force with the United States. Practically, the regime demanded the release of Iranian funds deposited in the U.S. back to the Ayatollahs and the remit of the Shah back to Tehran's authorities. Washington asked the Shah to leave and to instead live in Egypt where he later died. The Iranian funds were not released.

The hostage crisis was resolved as President Ronald Reagan took the White House, yet the confrontation between the two countries was maintained for decades. All ties were cut between Washington and Tehran, and the faces of the confrontation moved to several other countries, including Syria, Lebanon and eventually Iraq after the U.S. invasion of 2003.

Hostage taking in Lebanon: 1981 to 1988

After the U.S. embassy hostage crisis in Tehran in 1979, the Iranian regime engaged in Western hostage taking in Lebanon as well as major terrorist attacks there as part of its overall policy. The debut of Iranian direct military action in Lebanon was marked by twin suicide attacks in Lebanon against the French and American barracks, killing hundreds of soldiers and Marines. The massacre of Peace units dispatched to ensure the protection of Palestinian refugees and to secure the capital after the Israeli withdrawal of 1982 showed the extent of Khomeinist determination to obtain domination via extreme violence. The September 1983 terror attacks had no military logic for Iran, located hundreds of miles east of Lebanon. But the goals of such terror were to signify to the U.S. and the West that Lebanon was falling under Iran's zone of control. The Ayatollahs wanted the country to fall under Hezbollah's rule. The concerns of Tehran were that a Lebanese Army under secular and moderate leadership, and eventually a Lebanese government signing a Peace Treaty with Israel, would shatter the Islamic Republic's dreams of reaching the Mediterranean.

It was in this context of geopolitics that Tehran ordered the attacks against Western allies in Beirut. Iranian officials have publicly acknowledged that the ideology and the explosives that killed hundreds in Lebanon were imported from Iran. The suicide attacks against the U.S. and French militaries were followed with car bombs against the U.S. embassy and other targets. The use of car and truck bombs opened a new era in global Jihadi tactics. These methods were called "amaliyat istishadiya" ("suicide operations") by Hezbollah. They would become models to copy not just to other cells of Hezbollah, but also to Salafi Jihadists. In some of his statements, the leader of al Qaeda said after 9/11 that he "had observed Hezbollah in Lebanon in 1983, with one man, one truck killing hundreds of U.S. Marines." He concluded, "We've learned from them." Since then, suicide bombing became the principal tool for Jihadists worldwide.

The Iranian regime also ordered Hezbollah to kidnap American, French and British hostages to force Western governments to make concessions to the regime in both Lebanon and Iran. The sophistication with which the Iranian services operated was second only to the KGB. The hostages seized in Lebanon served as pawns in a secret chess match that included Western abandonment of the Iranian opposition. The strategy included kidnapping Western hostages in Lebanon, thus obtaining Western commitments to abandoning leaders and cadres from the Iranian opposition inside the country or overseas. One of the major results of this policy was the famous Iran-Contra Affair, a scandal where the U.S. attempted to discretely ship weapons from the Contras in Latin America to Iran in order to secure the release of the hostages. Gradually, Washington and European governments started to distance themselves from the Iranian opposition, particularly MEK, as a result of the hostage strategy. Iranian sponsored terror attacks on the streets of Paris also impacted the French government, which was engaged in talks about the MEK presence on French soil. In 1986, the government of Jacques Chirac agreed to and followed through on forcing MEK leaders to leave France.

Assad links up with Khomeini, axis forged

Meanwhile, in 1980, Iran's new regime received the visit of Hafez Assad, the Alawi dictator of Syria, who signed a mutual defense and cooperation treaty. At the root of this new axis was the sectarian identity of both Assad, representing the Alawis in power in Syria, and the Khomeinists, representing Jihadi Shiism in Iran. The alliance was forged in order to provide Assad strategic depth so he could break his isolation from the surrounding Arab Sunni regimes and could also provide Iran's regime with an entry point into the Arab world. The Khomeini-Assad axis is the oldest alliance in the Middle East. The vision of Khomeini and his successor Ali Khamenei and their apparatchik was to expand the Islamic Republic's influence, then dominance, west through Iraq's Shias, Syria's Alawites, and Lebanon's radicalized Shia, who would be led by Hezbollah. The Iranian-Syrian alliance established the foundation for expanding influence across the region. Cooperation began between the two intelligence services, and increasingly, the Iranian Revolutionary Guards (Pasdaran) were sent to Syria and from there to neighboring Lebanon to establish a nucleus of a Khomeinist-like military force: Hezbollah.

The radical Shia organization based in Lebanon was directly linked to the Supreme Leader's office in Iran. Hezbollah's secretaries-general became an integral part of the regime leadership in the Islamic Republic. Hezbollah spread in the northern Bekaa for two years before they launched their first deadly attacks on the U.S. and French Marines in Lebanon in 1983.

Iran's regime double wins in the post-Cold War era

As the Soviet Union was crumbling, the Islamic Republic was rising. Two dramatic geopolitical events elevated Tehran's regime to a higher and more powerful position in the balance of power in the region, and later worldwide. First, Saddam's invasion of Kuwait in August of 1990. The consequences of this war profited the Iranian regime immensely: Iran's threat was perceived as a lesser one compared to an openly devastating invasion of Kuwait by Iraq; Tehran received many jets flown by Iraqis to hide from Western strikes; the Shia inside Iraq felt empowered and rose against Saddam, only to be crushed militarily. But the suppression of Iraqi Shia in the south sent waves of their cadres across the borders into Iran, where the regime hosted them and transformed them into the spearhead for its future penetration of Iraq years later after the U.S. invasion of 2003.

Second, an ally of Iran, Hafez Assad, received the highest dividend he could dream of since 1976: a green light by the U.S. administration in the person of Secretary of State James Baker to resolve the Lebanese crisis as a reward for Syria's participation in the Kuwait campaign. Assad, who had already occupied two thirds of Lebanon and backed Hezbollah in its advance towards the south of the country, seized this magical moment in 1990 and—with that green light from Washington—"solved" the crisis in Lebanon by invading the last resisting enclave known as East Beirut in October 1990. A new pro-Syrian government was established, Hezbollah received full support from the Vichy style Lebanese government, and Iran was indirectly co-ruling most of Lebanon, and certainly its constitutional and military institutions. The new Assad-dominated Lebanon opened its grounds officially to Hezbollah and the Pasdaran, who used the vast Lebanese diaspora around the world to further expand in several countries. The control of that small country also provided Iran's regime with solid ground from which to "confront Israel directly," a highly important slogan to the regime.

Pre 9/11 Iranian strategies

After the collapse of the Soviet Union, and the Kuwait war, the Iranian regime positioned itself as a leading force in the region, taking advantage of the rapidly changing international relations. On the one hand, Tehran's elite realized the ascending power of the United States worldwide as the sole power and the difficulty of maneuvering that came with the disappearance of the bipolar world. Thus, the post-Cold war strategies of Iran centered on two parameters.

One was to avoid a direct confrontation with the United States. Back in the 1980s, during a military incident in the Gulf, U.S. Navy assets demonstrated the devastating effects of its power against Pasdaran naval units, all destroyed by American strikes after an aggression by the Iranian forces. The long goal of the Iranian regime, in order to deny the U.S. the capacity of ultimately removing the regime by force, was to acquire the nuclear bomb. Even as India and Pakistan were working on acquiring the doomsday device for their own balance of power, Iran's strategic thinking was already evolving toward obtaining this weapon— though it would take a decade or two to make it reality. The 1990s would be wisely described as the calm before the storm (read hurricane) as the regime would demonstrate after 9/11.

The second parameter was to accelerate geopolitical advances and the spread of intelligence, security and terror networks in the region and worldwide. By joining forces with Assad's regime, backing Hezbollah in Lebanon, Hamas in Gaza, and using Lebanon and Syria's diaspora worldwide to set up cells, the Iranian Islamist regime was building a vast web of deterrence against the United States and the West. The idea was to play "moderate and reformer" to Western public opinion while setting up a lethal system of retaliation on all possible levels. The long-range goal was to build a force capable of deterring the West from striking at Iran's nuclear weapons system, even before it was built or unveiled. In other words, deterring the West from deterring Iran was a very sophisticated strategic construct.

The illusion of moderation: Strategic deception

In 1997, Mohammad Khatami was elected president under the illusion of moderation. He was called the "Mikhail Gorbachev of Iran." Many Western and regional concessions were made to him. One of the most dangerous concessions was about the core organized opposition. After Khatami insisted the U.S. designate the MEK as a terrorist organization, the Clinton administration gave in and included on its terror list the only group capable of effectively opposing Tehran's policies. Europe followed suit. Meanwhile Khamenei, the one with the real power, was pushing full steam ahead with domestic repression and regional and international terror buildup. The U.S. and the West wasted a full decade after the collapse of the Soviet Union, granting the Jihadi regime more time, more space and more trust. The worst of all Western policies was to strike at the organized opposition.

Expansion of Quds Force and regime's audacity

In the 1990s, while the West was hoping for a change following the death of Khomeini, to the contrary, the regime expanded its operation of exporting terrorism and fundamentalism. The West had difficulty understanding what was happening. In short, having lost their "fuehrer" Ayatollah Khomeini, the regime was weaker and more vulnerable. But the Iranian ruling elite concluded that the survival of the regime could not be secured except by racing toward expansion. Identical to National Socialism, fascism, and Bolshevism, their doctrine was that the survival of the Islamic republic depended upon a permanent revolution. In short, for Khomeinism to survive, it must always expand. It is important to realize the regime's meddling in other countries is not inspired by its strength, but by fear for its survival. This fear was due to its natural incompetence to meet the demands of it people on social, political, economic and individual spheres. Until 1988, the war with Iraq and the slogan of "liberating Jerusalem" was a survival pillar for the regime. After the war, a new crisis had to be produced.

From this perspective one can understand the need for a Quds Force. It was established not for the purpose of classical war, but for a terror war that would be permanent and directed against current and potential enemies. In any conventional war against the West or a coalition of Arab countries, the regime knew it would ultimately lose. The Iraq War taught the Islamic republic's leadership that a determined foe can stop them militarily even if that foe is smaller in size. The more lethal way to defeat their enemies resided in the method of creating a few terror organizations with the aim of expanding the regime's views and influence to Muslims in other countries. Iran's regime used the 1990s to further recruit among Shia and started recruitment among Sunnis as well. However, 9/11 shocked Iranian leaders and induced even greater fear, which was then exacerbated by the U.S. removal of the Taliban and Saddam Hussein. Khamenei and his Pasdaran would again apply their traditional doctrine of deception: play nice, deceive, maneuver and execute advances on the ground—a strategic feature of Stalinism.

On the eve of September 11: The strength of the regime

The Iranian regime was doing well on the eve of the September 11, 2001, attacks by al Qaeda on New York, Washington, D.C., and Pennsylvania. A quick review of the geopolitics of Iran's regime can easily reveal the state of affairs before the start of the War on Terror. As a result of the Kuwait war, Tehran reaped many benefits as argued earlier. Saddam was boxed in and weaker. He was no longer a threat to the Khomeinist regime. MEK was practically silenced militarily inside Iraq and thus omitted as an operational menace. Radical Shia militias Badr and SCIRI (Supreme Council of the Islamic Revolution in Iraq), exiled from Iraq, were trained inside Iran for the potential "return." Assad had seized most of Lebanon and empowered Hezbollah. Critically important was the silencing of the Iranian opposition abroad through the tightening of legal status. Last, the Quds Force was rapidly filtering across the region and penetrating several countries, creating an international web of deterrence against potential future counterstrikes.

But the regime was also concerned about several growing realities. To its east, the Taliban Jihadi forces had seized power in Kabul, bringing the Sunni extremist competitor to their borders, which could feed the ethnic unrest deep in the hearts of minorities, at least in Kurdistan, Ahwaz and Baluchistan. But the most concerning development was the rise of a youth movement inside the country, particularly on campuses, despite the "cultural revolution" (read repression). In 1999, a generalized student uprising took place across Iran's universities. This was a decade-early warning and prelude to the popular explosion of 2009. The regime, very conscious about the "deeper Iran" resentful of the Ayatollahs, reinforced the idea of a strategic weapon—nuclear first—to deter the outside world from backing the "reactionary forces on the inside." The more civil society showed signs of uprising, the more the Ayatollahs moved toward establishing the geopolitical dominance and a strategic weapons threat.

The last achievement by an Iranian ally before 9/11 was the march toward Israeli borders and the lionization of Hezbollah and its leader Hassan Nasrallah after Israel's withdrawal from the so-called "security zone" in south Lebanon. After more than two decades with a presence in the border areas in Lebanon, Israel pulled its forces inside its own borders and dismantled the local defense force known as the South Lebanon Army (SLA).

Hezbollah, according to military experts, was never able—as a militia—to seize positions from the SLA made of former Lebanese Army soldiers from all communities including Shia. The small SLA force was able to withstand the Khomeinist terror organization for years before it was dismantled by the Ehud Barak Government, itself pressured by the Clinton administration to let go of south Lebanon and its small defense force. Starting in May 2000, pro-Iranian forces reached the Lebanese Israeli borders and Tehran's Pasdaran officers were watching the "Zionist entity" with their own binoculars. Iran's Islamic Republic reached one of its peak moments—just before Osama bin Laden hit the twin towers and the Pentagon.

From Fantasy to Strategy

During the 1990s and as the millennium ended, the Iranian regime was readying itself for a strategic leap to the completion of a geopolitical cohesive bloc equipped with international terror networks and eventually with strategic weapons. The Khomeinist fantasy was to build a "Shia Jihadi" empire stretching from Beirut's southern suburb to the center of Afghanistan, from Yemen's Saada hills to the Awali Mountains in Syria. The ideological agenda of the original Islamic revolution launched by Khomeini wanted to assemble all Shia first, across the region's borders, to establish what they consider a legitimate Imamate. But beyond the so-called Shia Jihadi version of the Caliphate, Khomeini's world vision went beyond sectarian frontiers. He and his followers envisaged to correct Islamic history and bring back the line of Ahl al Bait (or the lineage of Prophet Mohammad) to the helm of the Muslim world. Similar to the Salafi Jihadists who want to bring back a Sunni Caliphate abolished by Mustafa Kamal Ataturk in Turkey in the 1920s, the Khomeinists want to restore an Islamic order lost due to battles fought in the 7th century AD/CE. In short, Khomeinism is about a totalitarian view linked to a historical vision, to be implemented in modern times. Salafism and Khomeinism are thus the two faces of contemporary Jihadism, one is Sunni and the other is Shia.

Just before the Jihadi-Salafi al Qaeda attacks on New York and Washington, the Jihadi Khomeinist regime was readying itself to engage in its last leaps to create the geopolitical space for their Imamate. Between Iran and Syria, the only passage to connect this strategic plateau from the Indian Ocean to the Mediterranean was Iraq. Assad and Khamenei were working on an Iraq plan years before the Bush administration invaded Iraq. The two allies were training opposition to Saddam, both Islamists and Baathists, but Syria and Iran could not simply march through Iraq without triggering an international and Arab Sunni reaction. The Iranian plans for Iraq, however, were ready for implementation in two versions: a direct intervention through a Shia uprising in the south followed by a joint intervention with Syria to penetrate the country—or through provoking a third-party intervention which could open the path for their own control. The U.S. invasion of Iraq in 2003—and the manner of its exit in 2011—provided the opening they were waiting for.

Taking advantage of the Obama administration's policy in the region, Iran through its Revolutionary Guards is meddling in other countries more than any other time in the past. It has currently as many as 70,000 IRGC forces and other militias affiliate with the IRGC in Syria. These forces are directly participating in the killings in Syria and have committed war crimes along with Assad's Army. As stated earlier the theocratic regime's aggressive policy in the region is due to its domestic vulnerability and means of creating a false balance of power. However, unlike in the past the heavy casualties in Syria for Iran and growing opposition at home to huge amount of money and resources being allocated to the Syrian war has the potential of turning the meddling in Syria into a quagmire for the Iranian regime. The change of administration in the US and the departure of Obama, whose central policy in the region was to work with Iran to curb its nuclear program, has increased the pressure on Khamenei.

In addition, the main Iranian opposition, MEK, has been delisted from terror lists both in the US and Europe and gained more support internationally, in particular in the US both among policy makers and also in the US Congress. Moreover, the presence of Prince Turki bin Faisal Al Saud in the annual gathering of NCRI supporters in Paris in July 2016 was also a significant change in the regional alliances. Therefore, while the situation in Iran is deteriorating and there are strong rumors about Khamenei's health, as well as a more determined Arab countries to stand up to the Iranian regime's aggressive moves; it seems that a new balance of power is being shaped. In these circumstances the policy of the new US Administration could be more decisive.

Walid Phares is an academic and a researcher. He lectures global strategy at the National Defense University in Washington and was President Donald Trump's advisor on foreign policy during the US election campaign.

A view of political history of contemporary Iran

François Colombet

In these early years of the new century, the prospects for the Middle East and for the rest of the world give cause for concern. In many countries, elections have just taken place, or are about to do so: such is the case in the USA, in France and in Germany. In all these countries, policy on Iran is or was an issue under discussion during the electoral campaigns. This is especially the case as President Hassan Rouhani is ending his term in office in August 2017. No-one knows – except probably the Supreme Leader – who will succeed him, or whether he will stay in office for another term. Also, one has to admit that what were called "the Arab revolutions" simply gave rise either to a strengthening of authoritarian States, or to the political breakdown of entire regions. Tunisia seems to be the only country in the region to have instituted a new, more-democratic, governance. In the Middle East, the states occupying the territories previously ruled over by the Western powers, in the former Turkish Empire, are in the process of breaking up. Such is the case in Iraq and Syria. In Africa, Libya practically no longer exists. In all these conflicts, the stronger neighboring states, such as Turkey and Iran, have pulled their chestnuts out of the fire, after, previously, having often fanned the flames. In addition, in Yemen, the Kurdistan region, and the Gulf States, all the ingredients are there for devastating conflicts in the short term, conflicts in which Iran is playing – or, in any case, is readying to play – its habitual role. How can one not be worried when one learns that diplomatic relations have recently been severed between Iran and Saudi Arabia? The pretext or opportunity for this break-off was the attacks on the Saudi Embassy in Tehran and its consulate in Mashhad after the execution, in January 2016, of a Shiite imam from Saudi Arabia. Furthermore, there is an on-going dispute between the two nations after a "disturbance" that occurred during the 2015 Mecca pilgrimage, during which several hundred Iranians were killed.

As was mentioned previously, Iran profited greatly from these problems and has been doing so for a long time. Khomeini's arrival in power was followed by violent confrontations, first with the USA and then with the rest of the world. The storming of the American embassy that gave rise to the failed American commando mission in Iran, the Supreme Leader's calls for a worldwide revolution, and the terrorist attacks in the West and in places as far away as Argentina have all been violent provocations contributing not inconsiderably to the problematic worldwide situation. The call for the death of Salman Rushdie – which it should not be forgotten was behind the murder of two of his editors – is the regime's standard call and has been used to incite many of the violent attacks against intellectuals that have darkened the early years of this millennium. One can understand that Khomeini's Iran has been shunned even though, as time goes by, trade dealings have resumed with a certain degree of caution.

Now, after the period of cold relations with the Westerners, Iran wants to get its frontiers reopened and restore trade relations. This is the much-anticipated effect of the agreement signed on July 14, 2015 in Vienna which – after long and laborious negotiations in which it should be remembered that France demonstrated more caution than the other partners – acknowledged Iran's renunciation of nuclear weapons. In their desire to welcome back this great nation which, so it seemed, had finally regained its senses, the signatories deliberately closed their eyes to the perverse role that Iran continues to play in Lebanon, Syria, Iraq and Yemen. This attitude of benevolence is continuing to endure. The shipment of arms from Iran to Yemen via an Iranian vessel in March 2016 and also during recent times the firing of ballistic missiles capable of carrying a nuclear warhead from Iranian territory were only formally protested against, with no sanctions applied by the UN. There was no question of spoiling the newly-restored relations.

Many personalities – heads of states, ministers, and members of parliament – have now traveled to Iran, as have businessmen. For its part, the government has let it be known that the country needs to renew a large part of its public amenities, and foreign contractors are going to be allowed to make bids. The oil company Total is now hoping to be able to exploit the gas reserves, Airbus wants to sell aircraft, and so on. But there are still many technical obstacles.

Not all sanctions against Iran have yet been lifted – particularly those imposed by the United States in 1979 for supporting terrorism and for human rights violations. The misadventures of non-American companies having concluded contracts in dollars and therefore being subject to checks and financial sanctions by the United States is understandably worrying lots of investors. The legal problems, the need to master a little-known language, the legal forms unfamiliar to a Westerner (like the big Iranian foundations), as well as the generalized corruption that has unknown aspects even for the most-experienced Westerners are all impediments to the restoration of trade relations. Nonetheless, many difficulties have been overcome, and the "slow recovery" – to use a term employed by a French pundit – does seem to be getting underway, although not as strongly as expected. However, for the moment, no-one can say what will happen next, as the situation in the Middle East and the rest of the world is currently unstable, especially since the government in power in Iran appears unreliable.

But there is one sector in which the recovery has taken hold quickly: tourism. It has notably been the case for the French, especially since the Foreign Ministry very quickly removed Iran from its list of high-risk countries. It is the general opinion of all having visited the country during 2015 and 2016 that the people are open and friendly, and the country is captivating. Iran actually has a rich archeological heritage that gives one an idea of its long history. It also has a strong identity, with a territory that has not changed, an original language, and abundant ancient and modern literature. In Persia, poetry has always been loved and practiced.

Iran is still characterized by the undeniably high profile of its religion which, since the 1979 revolution, has been the driving force of its political institutions. This is the land of Shiism, a variant that emerged at the beginning of Islam. However, the kingdom did not massively convert to Shiism until the sixteenth century, probably in opposition to the Sunni Turks. For the Shiites, the succession of the Prophet Mohammed should not have passed to his companions, but to his cousin, Ali, Caliph from 656 to 661, the date on which he was killed by a usurper. His descendants nearly all met the same dramatic fate. This is why the culture of martyrdom is an important aspect of Shiism. The twelfth and last of Ali's descendants to have left this cruel world is the "Invisible Imam", who is to return at the end of time. From this tragic history, the Shiites learned with certitude that all political power is impure and unjust. This refined and complex religion also has variants around the world. Iran is the leading light. It will be seen further on that these statements have their significance.

To return to the increasing numbers of tourists visiting Iran now, in the twenty-first century, what strikes them and attracts them the most is an apparently well-blended mix of both the past and modern life. In reality, probably because of the religious dictatorship in whose grips it is, the country has rather archaic aspects but was swept by a desire for modernity from the nineteenth century onwards. The Shahs of the time, and the major personalities and intellectuals, traveled widely. Frequent contacts with Britain, Russia, Germany and France led to the King of Persia being persuaded to experiment with a constitutional regime as from 1906. This form of government certainly did not last very long: the British, who were interested in the recently-discovered oil, and the Russians, whose prime objective was to acquire Iranian territory, helped the royalty to divest itself of this dangerous form of democracy. But the memory has remained vivid in the minds of modern Iranians. The "constitutional revolution" of 1906 is a point of reference and a major milestone in their history. Nearly all the revolutionary or reformist movements have drawn inspiration from it. For history, with its violence and its wars, has not overlooked Iran, and the great nation has lived its moments of collective pride. One was when, after a period of great confusion, Dr Mohammad Mossadegh came to power. He was a prime minister justifiably hostile to British colonialism and spoke to British embassy attachés in French. In 1951, to take action against the plundering of Iranian oil by Western companies, a resolution was adopted unanimously by the Parliament: nationalization of the oil. As might be expected, the British – with the help, this time, of the United States – fomented a plot against him. Mossadegh was overthrown in 1953, arrested, judged and sentenced and, after his imprisonment, would spend the rest of his life in surveilled accommodations. Even today, visits to his tomb are under strict control by the police.

There were attempts to modernize the country during the reign of the last Shah. The supposed reforms were forced through and were very unpopular. The government responded to the protest movements with violent repression. Despite having support from the West, the Shah's government only stayed in power through an omnipresent police apparatus that made arbitrary arrests, tortured and performed summary executions. It was at this time in history that a formidable political police was built-up with self-serving American help. The present government then inherited that police apparatus. Among the more positive things that survived from that period were the reforms benefiting women, whose status was considerably improved. Certainly, a large part of these achievements have been abolished by the mullahs, but there is one essential measure that remains in existence in Iran: women are allowed to take up teaching and many other professions. In truth, this accomplishment dates farther back: Iranian women started to become emancipated, and girls' education was modernized at the beginning of the century.

It is undoubtedly both to the persistence of the rich ancient culture and to the generally-available and good-quality education provided in Iran that the country owes its access to the most-refined forms of contemporary culture, notably its film industry. There is indeed a genuinely-Iranian school of film directors and producers, with great artists who win international prizes and have a big international audience, notably in France. Of course, a large part of their works are not screened in Iran, because censorship there is vigilant and only allows films compatible with the regime's ideology, or else propaganda movies. It is also because of this censorship that the Modern Art Museum of Tehran – an unmissable sight for tourists – no longer displays works by Picasso, Warhol, Bacon and many other artists. It was because of the mocking questions from Western art circles that an exhibition of such works was finally seen in Tehran. Even so, the exhibition of these works from abroad has been set back because, we are told, of the troubled context of the elections in Iran. The explanation is that Rouhani doesn't want to draw criticism from conservatives. Iran is in a paradoxical situation: behind the appearances of freedom and modern life, the country is in the grips of the most-backward obscurantism and the most-brutal tyranny.

The current regime dates back to 1979, when the Shah – who had previously been supported by the West – was overthrown by popular revolt. Originally, the most diverse schools of belief stood allied but, as a result of the difficulties in setting-up a Government of Union, the revolution was taken over by a figure from the Shiite hierarchy, which is extremely powerful within Iran, as explained above. Ayatollah Khomeini had fought against the Shah. He had then been sent to exile in Iraq, and then in France. But when he returned to Tehran, he was welcomed by millions of Iranians. Meanwhile, the Shah had fled abroad. Khomeini managed to have a referendum vote to accept the principle of an Islamic Republic, and commissioned a committee of theology specialists to write a constitution, working from a draft based on the French Constitution of 1958, and his own draft explained in a book that he had written during his exile, in which he recounted his conception of *Velayat-e-faqih*, the doctrine by which supreme authority has to be entrusted to a Religious Advisor recognized by the people as the representative of the Hidden Imam.

The constitution voted for makes provisions for a legislative power exercised by one single assembly elected by universal suffrage. Executive power is then entrusted to a President of the Republic, who is also elected by universal suffrage for four years. In the initial version of the Constitution, a Prime Minister was provided for. The Constitution would be less unconventional if there was not one all-powerful figure above the executive and the legislature: the "Supreme Leader of the Islamic Revolution" – in other words, "the Religious Advisor representing the Hidden Imam" in the theory of *Velayat-e-faqih*. Article five of the Constitution deserves to be quoted insofar as, with regard to the Supreme Leader, it explicitly refers to the Shiite religion: "during the time of concealment of His Holiness the Imam of the Period ... the executive regency and the direction of the Islamic community of believers ... belong to the Religious Advisor, who is just, virtuous, cognizant with the problems of the time, courageous, capable of leading, able to advise...", pointing out that Khomeini himself was "recognized and accepted by a decisive majority as religious leader and guide" (Article 107 of the 1989 draft of the Constitution). This divine origin does indeed give the Leader powers that are veritably "supreme", allowing him to "confirm" the President – notwithstanding the fact that the President is elected by universal suffrage – and giving him the right to dismiss the President. The Leader controls the judiciary, radio and television. He is the Marshal of all branches of the Armed Forces, and personally appoints their Commander in Chief. He also controls very many influential religious organizations, such as those for Friday prayers, etc. Thus, the President of the Republic – who theoretically holds the executive power – only does so under the Leader's tight control. As for Parliament, all its work is screened by the "Guardian Council of the Constitution" provided for in Article 72 of the Constitution, having 12 members, six of whom are chosen by the head of the judiciary, who himself is appointed by the Leader and elected by the Parliament. The other six are appointed directly by the Supreme Leader. These are the six that examine whether the texts voted for by the Parliament are in conformity with Sharia or not. Otherwise said, all laws are subject to the approval of the Leader or his representatives. The Guardian Council also has the power of accepting or rejecting a candidature for elections. So one can only stand for an election if one is approved by the Leader.

Khomeini took advantage of the situation of revolt to impose the first Leader. But the successor he had considered – Ayatollah Hossein-Ali Montazeri, who was a past companion with whom he had worked on what was then only a draft constitution – had opposed him and criticized his decision taken in 1988 to have many opponents executed, particularly students and women, of whom many who were in prison and were in the process of serving a sentence. The implementation of a constitutional reform that would be voted for shortly after the death of Khomeini in December 1989, would enable his successor to be appointed, by founding an "assembly of experts for the selection of the Leader" responsible, as its name suggests, for choosing the Supreme Leader. These experts are certainly elected by universal suffrage, but to stand as candidate in an election, you have to be a cleric faithful to the Leader, and must be authorized by the Guardian Council to stand, following a very-restrictive procedure. This same 1989 reform would abolish the Prime Minister, whose role would now be fulfilled by the President of the Republic, who nonetheless does not hold the role of "coordination of powers", a function that is fulfilled by... the Supreme Leader (Article 57). Another reform was that to settle any conflicts between the Parliament and the Guardian Council, a "council of discernment of the government's interest" (otherwise known as the State Expediency Council) was formed, with the members being appointed by the leader himself. All these measures had the common effect of further increasing the already-exorbitant powers of the Supreme Leader.

After Khomeini's death, a new Leader, Ali Khamenei, was chosen, who continued to use all the possibilities of the Constitution. So, when desires for a softening of the government started to be expressed, the Constitution enabled the Supreme Leader to orient the reformist voters towards a candidate compatible with the government's interests while presenting the appearance of moderation. Mohammad Khatami was elected, someone who offered all the necessary assurances in this respect. He had been a minister during the Khomeini period, notably at the time of the executions in 1988. When elected President, he approved the repression of student demonstrations, while allowing the passage of reformist laws such as a law abolishing torture in prison. The Guardian Council declared these laws not to be in conformity with the Quran. The Leader refrained from calling on the State Expediency Council. So the laws voted for were not enacted.

The meager achievements of the Khatami presidency (1997-2005) are worthy of comment for two issues: under his presidency, Westerners believed that the regime was changing from within, thanks to this moderate President, moving towards a more-democratic model, and therefore complacently satisfied the government's demands to repress its opponents who had become refugees in the West, which was a violation of the right to asylum. Subsequent events also showed that, during this period, although the Iranian government had officially suspended its nuclear program in 1979, during the Khomeini period, and although it had signed a technical cooperation program agreement with the IAEA in 1997, and then signed a further agreement in 2003, after being suspected of having enriched uranium, it had in reality secretly continued its program to acquire nuclear weapons expertise.

The period that follows started with the election of a new President who would serve a very important role for two terms of office. Mahmoud Ahmadinejad wasn't a cleric, he was a militia man from one of the groups that the regime originally formed to duplicate the Army, which was suspected of being loyal to the Shah, and of undertaking special operations. These militias were frequently used to maintain order in Iran, as well as for dark purposes such as eliminating opponents, including those abroad. Sometimes these henchmen used Iran's embassies as base camps, involved in cases having been placed under investigation in the West. They played an important role in the organizing of oil trafficking. They were involved in the nuclear field. In short, Ahmadinejad was the perfect representative for the lines of support of the most faithful to the Islamist regime. Right from his arrival in power, he adopted a firm attitude on foreign provocation, and would contribute to souring the nuclear issue. It was mentioned above that, since 1979, the United States had been applying sanctions. In 2005, the UN and the European Union also enforced sanctions. And, in 2009, after Ahmadinejad's re-election, the sanctions were further hardened.

Iran stood isolated during this period. Many Iranian opponents took asylum in the West. The regime hoped to get rid of the most effective by getting them convicted in Western courts. But these opponents – including members of the PMOI, managed to avoid the convictions and the applicable penalties. Several times, international organizations and associations drew attention to the systematic violations of freedoms taking place in Iran. It should be noted that, apart from the Constitution explained earlier, the regime also had a legal system and legislation that enabled it to conduct a veritable reign of terror. The judges, whose role is of a religious nature, were under the control of the Supreme Leader. The legislation applied was taken from the Quran, and the laws adopted by Parliament were under the supervision of the Guardian Council, as well as being controlled through *fatwas* from the Supreme Leader. We already said that Ayatollah Montazeri blamed Khomeini for having ordered the execution of many prisoners, through a *fatwa*. It is noteworthy that Iran's penal system that allows the use of torture also does not assign the same strength to the testimony of a woman as to that of a man. So, if the offense is punishable by beating, or by death by stoning, it must be proved by testimony "from four just men, or three just men and two just women". Criminal laws provide for many forms of corporal punishment, as well as for death, torture, beating and, in certain cases, stoning, and even crucifixion, etc. And these penalties are applied. According to observers and information from the Iranian government itself, Iran is – proportionally to its population – the country where death sentences are applied most often. Executions often take place in public, by hanging the victim from a crane, which slowly hoists the victim up until he or she is hanging with legs kicking above the crowd. This spectacle – one might even call it a show – is obviously designed to sow fear in the population. The kinds of people being condemned to death are government opponents and common law criminals, including many petty drug dealers. Iran continues to apply the death penalty for minors, even though it has ratified a convention abolishing capital punishment for minors.

Many people had hoped that at the end of the second term of President Ahmadinejad, who was replaced in August 2013 by Hassan Rouhani – presented as a moderate – human rights would be better respected in Iran. This has not been the case. However, as soon as this "moderate" new President was elected, dialogue was resumed with the West, and gave rise to the Vienna nuclear agreement of July 14, 2015. This agreement cannot hide the fact that in the past, and ever since Khomeini came to power, Iran has been constantly involved in armed conflicts in the region and that it is now openly taking part in wars in Iraq and Syria. And this – let it be repeated – is just after it has signed an agreement of reconciliation with the West.

The border regions of Iraq, where the holy sites of Shiism are to be found, have always attracted the Iranians. When the United States overthrew Saddam Hussein's regime, which was governing by the Sunnis, with the influence of Kurd and Christian minorities, they gave power to the Shiites. Some of the new Iraqi leaders the Americans put into power in Baghdad were even trained in… Tehran. The Sunni government employees – particularly military personnel – were dismissed and replaced by Shiites. It was a gift from the United States, offering Iraq to Iran. It also gave the violent Sunni opposition fully-trained leadership personnel! Yet it was not certain that the dictatorship of the mullahs actually wanted a successful democratic republic on its frontier, let alone a successful democratic republic as conceived by the Americans, even if it was a Shiite one. Moreover, at that time, they had plenty of other worries, and the accomplishment of a democratic Iraq seemed pretty illusory. In any case, in Iraq, as in Syria, there is an established involvement of Iranian militias. A recent report from the UN says that during May 2016, Iranian IRGC General Qassem Soleimani was present in the country. He is a heavyweight figure in the regime and is on the list of persons banned by the UN from traveling.

In Syria, Iran has long been on the side of the Assad regime, the members of which are themselves from the Alawite minority – a distant form of Shiism. The Shiite Hezbollah, which Iran had previously helped get rooted in Lebanon, would serve as an additional militia at the service of the Syrian government in its fight against a part of its population in revolt. Because of the extent to which the conflict flared, officers and undoubtedly troops brought in directly from Iran have fought on the side of the Syrian regime's forces. At the end of the siege of the city of Aleppo, the Iranians were even able to impose their own conditions, delaying the evacuation until protection was provided for sites occupied by Shiite militia allies. Even so, Iran was kept out of a central role in the peace negotiations.

Nearly 40 years ago, Ayatollah Khomeini preached holy war in the name of all Islam, and his words were heard throughout the Islamic world. However, over the years, this holy war of Islam has become the Shiites' war. All the close minorities are involved. This is the case in Lebanon, Yemen, in the Gulf States, and elsewhere in the world. Sunni states have been worried about it for a long time, especially as – here and there in Sunni territory – one hears about Muslims having apparently converted to Shiism. It is difficult to know the extent of the phenomenon, particularly as Shiism authorizes concealment in such cases. This expansion of Shiism explains the growing hostility of the Gulf monarchies. President Obama's behavior probably also played a role. During the war against Iraq, he opposed President Bush. Elected President of the United States and obviously wanting to score a success through negotiations, even if only to achieve more than his predecessors, Obama was supportive of Iran during the nuclear negotiations. Plus, like a counterpoint to that, didn't Obama also severely reprimand the Gulf monarchies for their support of certain terrorists? Another sign – if one was needed – of the increase in dangers in the region is that some observers have noted the beginning of a rapprochement between Saudi Arabia and Israel to counter Iranian activism (Le Monde, January 23, 2016). But President Obama's term has ended. The near future will depend, in particular, on the behavior and choices of the new American administration. Do we need reminding that, before his election,

Donald Trump was highly critical of the Vienna nuclear deal?

The near future will also depend on the issue of the armed conflicts in the Middle East, in which there are big nations involved like Russia, Turkey, France and the US, as well as – more discreetly but still closely – Saudi Arabia, Qatar, Lebanon, Jordan, and Israel. One can surmise that new coalitions may take form. Iran is still a heavyweight puncher. Another unknown is the result of the upcoming elections in Iran. We already know that the Supreme Leader seems to have dissuaded Mahmoud Ahmadinejad from standing again. Does that mean he will keep "moderate" Rouhani, or will he impose a hardliner like General Soleimani (who it seems is being talked about in Tehran) or else Ebrahim Raisi, whose track-record includes his involvement in the 1988 massacre of political prisoner? His choice will doubtlessly depend on the message he wants to send to his people and to his Western "partners". It's undeniable that since the emergence of the Islamic Republic in Iran, presidents have always been chosen according to the policy being implemented by the Leader, according to the image of Iran that he wants to put across. It's always a game of masks, and sometimes a game of charades. "Moderate" presidents have frequently been used to dissimulate practices that had nothing moderate about them. When looking at the nuclear issue previously, we saw that Iran has often deliberately lied to the international community.

In another domain, the prevention of terrorism – something which is a concern for most countries – one could admire the deftness with which this regime, of which the founder and first Supreme Leader called for holy war and violent terrorism, is now presenting itself as an adversary of the Islamic State, whereas it has not itself renounced Islamist terrorism: the *fatwa* against Salman Rushdie was never revoked and has been adopted by the present Supreme Leader. More anecdotally but no less significantly, you can now see advertisements in the Tehran press to recruit and train "forces in quest of martyrdom" – in other words, people ready to commit suicide in kamikaze acts. These adverts are headed by a quote from "His Eminence, the Supreme Leader, Ayatollah Ali Khamenei": "In the name of God the most high, martyrdom operations incarnate the summit of greatness of the nation and the apogee of its epic journey". This is so perverse: this regime, which calls people to terrorism and has employed it on occasions, uses the supposed danger that it causes to sow fear in its population. The police and Revolutionary Guards regularly arrest, with lots of publicity, individuals alleged to be Daesh members readying themselves "to go into action". It is the opinion of all the specialists that these are just operations mounted by the police authorities for propaganda purposes. In that way, the regime can present itself as a victim of Islamic State – which, paradoxically, has never really targeted Iran, whereas it does not hesitate to strike in countries as far away as France.

But careful scrutineers of the history of the Islamic Republic of Iran will observe something else: the Islamic institutions are simply the cladding for what is truly a totalitarian State, controlled by a small group of Shiite clerics and their collaborators. In other contexts, Islam has shown that it can be compatible with democracy. But, not here. One might imagine that after the violent period of the revolution, the governance would be more humane. But there are no changes to be seen in human rights. The capital punishment of minors, accepted inequalities of treatment between men and women, and violations of public freedoms are just the same.

In short, this regime is everything contrary to a democratic one. The new President of the French Republic will have to bear this in mind. But while this regime is detestable, the Iranian people merit admiration and trust. Once again, its level of culture, will bring their rewards in the future. We can look back at what Barack Obama said about countries that neglect the education of their youth, thus delivering them into the hands of the terrorists. One can also remember Tunisia again, where – like in Iran – everyone,

131

boys and girls alike, go to school, and that this has been the case for several generations, thanks to a voluntarist policy. But in Tunisia, it's the women – including those belonging to religious parties – who have prevented undesirable developments. Iranian women are certainly able to fulfill the same role.

Let's add a little anecdote to the commentary earlier about the cinema domain in Iran: the government made some propaganda films about the Islamic revolution and covered the Iran-Iraq war, which lasted practically throughout the Khomeini era. Khomeini knew that the state of war enabled him to keep tight control over the population in the name of the national interest, and he deliberately made the conflict last until 1988. But, instead of seeing the Leader's governance as worthy of praise, younger adults actually asked some annoying questions: why did the war last so long, with its thousands of dead and wounded, when Iraq was asking for peace? Why were there massive executions of opponents, particularly young students accused of being members of the People's Mujahedin (PMOI or MEK)? In short, the discussion gravitated to the historic recital. At the beginning of the year, university students even publically questioned parliament members about this terrible period in their history, and it was broadly covered on the social networks. The murders of young Iranians ordered by Khomeini in 1988 are part of a buried past that is coming back to the light, to the point at which one association requested the UN to review the matter again to see whether a case should be filed with the International Criminal Court.

We know that it was precisely about these massacres that Ayatollah Montazeri criticized Khomeini at the time for his murderous *fatwa*. But Montazeri's son recently took the courageous step of publishing the letter that his father wrote to the Supreme Leader, with the recording of a conversation between them that he had kept. To start with, Montazeri's son was charged and condemned to twenty-something years in jail! Then, faced with the questions the affair was arousing, faced with this re-opening of a shameful episode at the beginning of the Islamic Republic, and faced with the exposure of the cruelty done in the name of Islam, the regime beat a retreat and ultimately suspended the sentence for Montazeri's son. It was doubtlessly a smart move, but demonstrated that public opinion is no longer accepting the regime's wicked acts. May the questions being asked by young people – to whom the future belongs – give us hope for change, even though the regime manages to stay in power by dramatizing the dangers of terrorism and laying claim to the necessity of wars. One can no longer really talk about national cohesion. In reality, there is an urgent need to improve living conditions in the country, relieve unemployment and address the ecological emergency: As a good demagogue, Ahmadinejad authorized the drawing of water from many rivers, which have now dried up. Tehran is one of the most polluted cities in the world. Yet, to improve people's living conditions – or, at least, to give the impression that it wants to do so – the regime needs international aid. In other words, it needs the West.

In our country, awareness is an ancient tradition, even though some – such as the Foreign Ministry – have encountered a defeatist attitude, most of the elected representatives of the French people have opted for a clear line. Thus, the Parliamentary Committee for a Democratic Iran – which has many members from the National Assembly, of all persuasions, and is chaired jointly by a Republican and a Socialist – has always said that "The improvement of the human rights situation in Iran must be a prerequisite to any development of diplomatic and trade relations with the government in power in Tehran, and these improvements must be measurable through a halt in executions, the release of political prisoners, and respect for freedom of expression and association… At this time when Iran needs economic relations with the West more than ever, a realistic policy towards this country can only be based on an equilibrium that takes account of the Iranian people's calls for democracy, with no reason to think that they would actually benefit from an economic openness in the country when the different factions – notably the Revolutionary Guards – have every intention of enjoying the advantages."

All this must be remembered by our future President of the Republic, and by the new members of the French National Assembly and the new civil service staff who will be handling international portfolios. Iran is a country inhabited by a civilized and modern people but is under the reign of an obscurantist and totalitarian regime. France and its representatives must demand that the regime respect human rights, abolish torture and capital punishment, and practice gender equality, as Iran has as much to gain – or even more than we do – from close economic relations with our country.

François Colcombet is the President of the Foundation for the Middle Eastern Studies, Honorary Magistrate, former Advisor to the Court of Cassation and Co-Founder of the Magistrates' Syndicate

Military dimension, the hidden face of the Iranian nuclear program

Alejo Vidal-Quadras

Introduction

A year and a half after the July 2015 agreement between the major powers (P5 + 1) and Iran on Iran's controversial nuclear program, the international community expected that with the implementation of this agreement and inspections of all the sites of the Iranian regime, the outstanding questions about the military dimensions of this program would find answers or at least some of them would be clarified.

But a year and a half later, the essential questions remain unanswered and important ambiguities and doubts continue to subsist on the military intentions of the program.

The problem is due to the fact that for thirty-three years, the mullahs' nuclear activities were conducted by the Revolutionary Guards (IRGC) who aimed at the acquisition of the atomic bomb. The military aspect of this program remained hidden behind a civilian program screen presented by the Atomic Energy Organization of Iran (AEOI). The outward appearance was conducting research for atomic energy while the heart of this program was animated by the operation of a "Revolutionary Guards' Research Center" that was seeking to acquire the bomb.

135

Several IRGC officers were the key figures in this project and continue their activities. The central body has since changed its name and is called the Organization for New Defense Research (Sazman-e pazhouhesh-haye novine defai - SPND). A year and a half after the agreement, this center continues to exist.

That is why it is useful to look at the nature of Iran's nuclear program, which may have been partly halted but not dismantled by the agreement.

The issue of the Iranian regime's secret nuclear program and its drive to acquire nuclear weapons has been one of the major global security concerns of the new millennium. Tehran's continuous lack of cooperation and its deliberate and elaborate schemes to prevent the International Atomic Energy Agency (IAEA) from complete and free access to its program has deeply aggravated the problem. The IAEA is the UN agency in charge of surveillance of nuclear proliferation, in other words, the eyes and ears of the international community on these issues.

While the issue of the Iranian nuclear weapons program was sporadically discussed in the 1990s, the issue made international headlines and became a pressing issue subsequent to major disclosures by the prominent Iranian opposition, the National Council of Resistance of Iran, which exposed the secret enrichment site of Natanz and the heavy water reactor in Arak in August 2002. The subsequent NCRI revelations, based on information obtained and compiled by the network of the People's Mojahedin Organization of Iran (PMOI/MEK), shed light on various heretofore unknown aspects of the Iranian nuclear program.

Since this date, the IAEA has continuously and with different degrees of success, has kept this program under surveillance in order to detect a highly protected secret, that is, the existence of an underground program aimed at the acquisition of a nuclear bomb.

In November 2011, the IAEA provided its most extensive findings of "possible military dimensions" (PMD) of the Iranian nuclear program. The annex to the November 2011 report set the benchmark for assessing the secret aspects of the Iranian regime's nuclear program.

The issue of PMD was rightly so at the heart of major questions regarding the nature and objective of the Iranian nuclear program and the consequent policy and approach.

In November 2014, as the nuclear negotiations between Iran and the P5+1 gained momentum, the International Committee In Search of Justice (ISJ), a Brussels-based international NGO, conducted an exhaustive research on the question of the PMD of the Iranian nuclear program.

The report drew on all IAEA reports since 2003 (the year in which Iran's clandestine nuclear program was placed under the spotlight following the revelation of secret sites at Natanz and Arak by the NCRI in 2002), on reports by the Iranian opposition, and on studies and reports by credible think thanks and non-governmental organizations and thus provided a review of the most prominent and most essential aspects of the question, the military aspect. Turning a blind eye to these aspects will make it easier for the Iranian regime to continue this program which, after all, has always been a clandestine project.

Important findings of the ISJ study

The study established that two parallel systems have been fully functional during the whole period of the development of this program: a civilian system that includes AEOI and universities; while a military system constitutes the secret aspect of this program. These two structures resemble two concentric circles, working in tandem. Over the years, the military part of the program has gone through reorganization or name changes but has moved forward including recent activities. According to available information, records, and documents, the military aspect of the program has been and remains at the heart of Iran's nuclear activities.

In this study, ten of the primary issues that are among the most important aspects of the PMD of the Iranian nuclear program are scrutinized. These are among the most important issues that the IAEA has been pursuing over the years, on which it has sought answers directly from Iran.

The 10 topics under review are:

- Existence of a thorough infrastructure called SPND (in charge of weaponization);
- Procurement of dual purpose equipment and their possible use for military dimensions of the nuclear program;
- Secret enrichment of uranium;
- Enrichment using laser technology;
- High explosives tests and trigger mechanism;
- Neutron initiator;
- Manufacturing uranium metal (uranium hemisphere);
- Hydro-dynamic tests and explosion vessels at Parchin site;
- Research on a nuclear warhead;
- A great number of key scientists and researchers engaged in PMD of the nuclear program;

None of the main topics of dispute with Iran have been completely resolved. Even if some issues seemed to have been close to resolution at some stage, the emergence of new information generated new concern about the same issues. Meanwhile Tehran on several occasions tried to create the impression that all matters of concern had been resolved and that the time had come to close the nuclear file.

The ISJ report came to each of the following conclusions

• Tehran has worked systematically on all the necessary aspects of obtaining nuclear weapons, such as enrichment, weaponization, warheads, and delivery vehicles at some stages. In other words, Iran has worked on specific programs and projects to master all necessary aspects of obtaining a nuclear weapon.

• The Iranian regime has been working on five specific projects for enrichment in various quantities and methods (Natanz, Arak, Lashkar-Abad, Shian, and Fordow). Tehran did not provide the IAEA with information on any of these sites and projects, much less at early stages or on its own initiative. As a pattern and in a systematic manner, the Iranian regime admitted to the existence of these sites only after their existence and activities were brought to the international community's attention by other sources, namely the Iranian opposition, and after the IAEA began to persist in requesting access to these sites.

• An important finding of the ISJ study reveals that two parallel systems have been fully functional during the whole period of the negotiations begun in 2003: a civilian system includes the AEOI and universities, while a military system constitutes the secret aspect of this program. These two structures function like two concentric circles, working in tandem. The military aspect of the program has been and remains at the heart of Iran's nuclear activities.

• The civilian section of the program has provided a very suitable and plausible conduit for procuring and obtaining dual-purpose technology and equipment ultimately used in the military section. A significant portion of the equipment for the military aspect has been obtained and procured under this guise. Some bodies at the highest level of the Iranian regime, including offices and centers affiliated with the President's Office have all been involved in smuggling or skirting sanctions to obtain illicit or dual-purpose equipment for these projects.

• Scores of senior officials of the two parallel systems have exchanged positions and responsibilities over the years. It has been common practice to utilize scientists and researchers in the civilian sector for the military program and to lend staff from the military sector to the civilian program in order to increase their proficiency and expertise by working on each other's facilities and centers before returning to their initial sectors of activity. Universities affiliated with the IRGC and the Ministry of Defense act as a bridge between these two programs and have played a major role.

• Scores of the personnel involved in Tehran's nuclear program are from the military, particularly from the command structure of the IRGC. This study noted several pieces of information indicating that the IRGC commanders have been involved in the nuclear program from its early stages. A number of the most senior officers and top brass of the IRGC have been following this project over the years.

• Various equipment and devices that were imported and purchased ostensibly for universities remain unaccounted for and the real purpose of the equipment remains undetermined.

• Iran has consistently sought and obtained the know-how and expertise from foreign nationals and nuclear weapons experts. This includes networks of international smugglers such as AQ Khan and individual experts from the former republics of the Soviet Union. This has provided invaluable assistance to the military dimension of Iran's nuclear program.

• The geographic locations of the centers engaged in design and research aspect of the program, including Mojdeh site (aka Lavizan 2), Shian site (Lavizan 1), and Imam Hossein University are located at the east of Tehran and the facilities involved in working on nuclear warheads, such as Hemmat, Parchin, and Metfaz sites are all located in the military zone in eastern Tehran. The proximity of these sites clearly illustrates the relationship between the bodies and centers involved in manufacturing nuclear weapons.

ISJ reiterated that its study can only lead to the conclusion that Iran has vigorously pursued its ambitions to obtain nuclear weapons. No serious indications that Tehran has halted or abandoned this project or intends to do so were observed.

On the contrary, all the available information pointed to the conclusion that Tehran has resorted to further concealment to keep its program intact and unhindered.

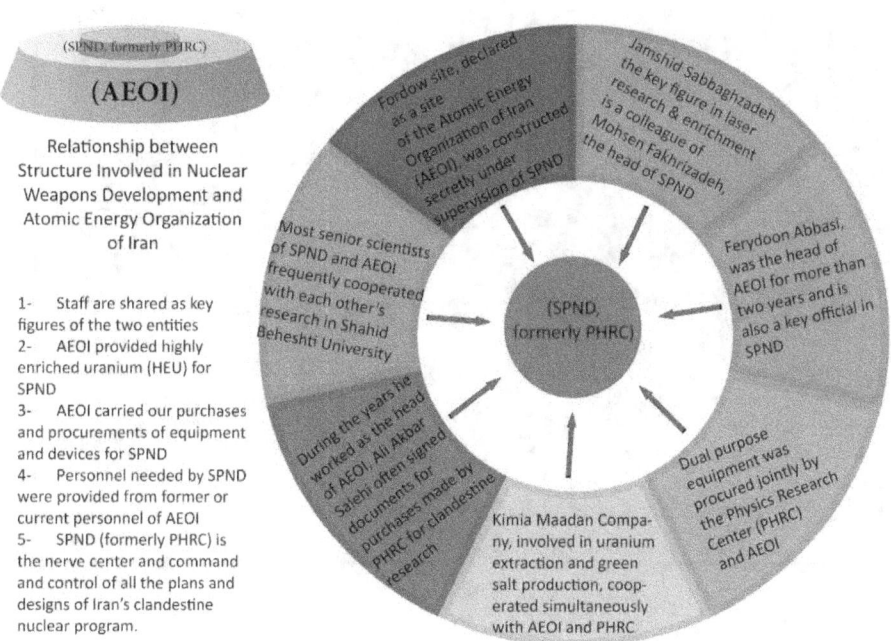

Relationship between Structure Involved in Nuclear Weapons Development and Atomic Energy Organization of Iran

1- Staff are shared as key figures of the two entities
2- AEOI provided highly enriched uranium (HEU) for SPND
3- AEOI carried our purchases and procurements of equipment and devices for SPND
4- Personnel needed by SPND were provided from former or current personnel of AEOI
5- SPND (formerly PHRC) is the nerve center and command and control of all the plans and designs of Iran's clandestine nuclear program.

Fordow site, declared as a site of the Atomic Energy Organization of Iran (AEOI), was constructed secretly under supervision of SPND

Jamshid Sabbaghzadeh the key figure in laser research & enrichment is a colleague of Mohsen Fakhrizadeh, the head of SPND

Most senior scientists of SPND and AEOI frequently cooperated with each other's research in Shahid Beheshti University

(SPND, formerly PHRC)

Ferydoon Abbasi, was the head of AEOI for more than two years and is also a key official in SPND

During the years he worked as the head of AEOI, Ali Akbar Salehi often signed documents for purchases made by PHRC for clandestine research

Kimia Maadan Company, involved in uranium extraction and green salt production, cooperated simultaneously with AEOI and PHRC

Dual purpose equipment was procured jointly by the Physics Research Center (PHRC) and AEOI

141

Relations of primary organizations involved in Iranian nuclear program

AEOI: Atomic Energy Organization of Iran
IRGC: Iran Revolutionary Guards Corps
MoD: Ministry of Defense
SPND (PHRC): Structures Involved
in Nuclear Weapons Development

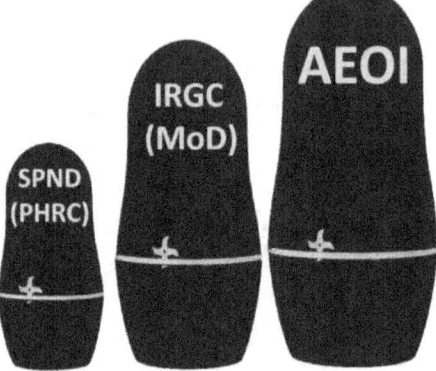

Concentration of key sites involved in military related nuclear activities in East Tehran

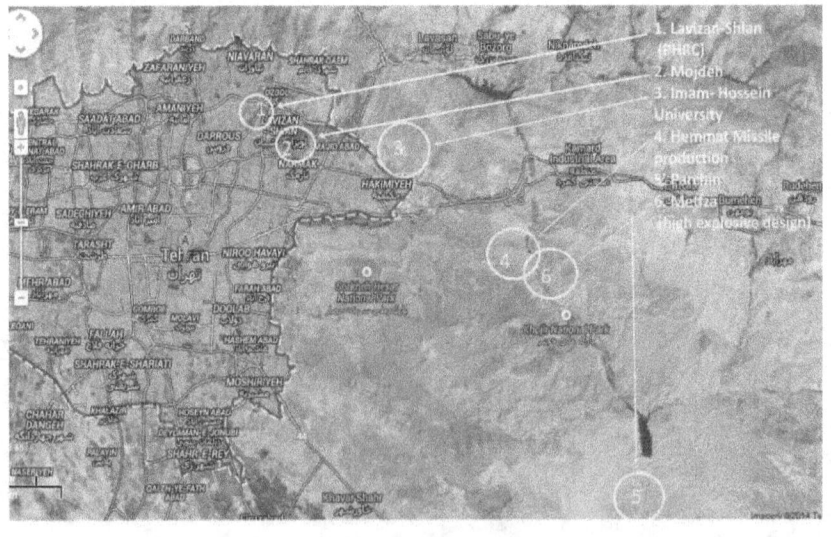

Evolution of the entity in charge of manufacturing nuclear weapons:

We have today an illuminating overview of evolution of the entity in charge of manufacturing nuclear weapons.

The regime's structures that have been focused on building a nuclear weapon during the past three decades have gone under various names and different forms, all seeking a specific goal of obtaining the necessary technology for making an atomic bomb. These structures have at various times been forced to change locations or even change the organization of their work due to revelations regarding their activities, or as a result of circumstances affecting the regime as a whole. However, through all these years of change, key personnel have remained fixed.

The various structures involved in nuclear weapons development were consolidated into a new entity, the Organization for New Defense Research (SPND), in 2011. Organized and focused under this new entity, those structures have officially become a department of the Ministry of Defense. The regime continues to refuse to provide any information to the IAEA regarding this entity, its research, or its personnel, some of who are extremely sensitive personnel for the regime's nuclear projects.

In 1983, Tehran launched a strategic research project within and overseen by the IRGC (Pasdaran) on nuclear technology for military purposes. In 1986, the IRGC opened nuclear research branches in numerous Iranian universities, with the most important being in Tehran University, Sharif University of Technology and Shiraz University. The IRGC has employed a number of physics graduates from Sharif University of Technology.

Following the end of the Iran-Iraq war in 1989, all activities and experts of the IRGC nuclear research center were transferred to the Physics Research Center, chaired by Seyed Abbas Shahmoradi

Zavare'i, an IRGC member, a university professor, and a member of the Jahad Research Center of Sharif University of Technology.

The center of this entity and its associated organizations were in a site in Tehran named the Physics Research Center in the Iranian capital's Lavizan-Shian region.

Turning point: Revelation of Lavizan-Shian as a site focusing on WMD production

On May 15, 2003, the National Council of Resistance of Iran unveiled new information on WMDs in Iran and exposed the Lavizan-Shian site in the Shian region. This was a turning point regarding international understanding of this entity and its activities.

Following the revelation of this location, aerial imagery showed that the regime had completely razed the Lavizan–Shian site and destroyed its buildings in March 2004. As a result, the IAEA inspectors sought to visit the site to ascertain the reason for the destruction.

The revelation and destruction of this site marked the beginning of major changes to the organization in charge of weaponization of the Iranian nuclear program.

Changing location of Lavizan–Shian to Mojdeh under the name of "New Defense Technology and Advanced Preparation Center"

On November 19, 2004, the NCRI reported that the center for weaponization of Iran's nuclear program had been transferred to a new site, with an area of around 60 acres. This new site with three gates on Mojdeh Avenue thus came to be identified as the Mojdeh site, or Lavizan 2 site. All Shian activities were transferred to this new center.

IRGC Brigadier General Seyed Ali Hosseini-Tash, the Deputy Minister of Defense, followed up on the nuclear activities with the IRGC staff member, Mohsen Fakhrizadeh, while biological weapons activities were followed up by another IRGC staff member, Nader Maghsoudi. Due to the top secret nature of this work, Ali Hosseini-Tash followed up on his activities directly with the then Defense Minister Ali Shamkhani. Mohsen Fakhrizadeh, a renowned Ministry of Defense expert, was in charge of the New Defense Technology and Advanced Preparation Center. This center was formerly the entity providing logistics and backup for the Ministry of Defense's ammunition production. Upon an order by Defense Minister Ali Shamkhani, the evacuation of Shian-Lavizan had begun 18 months earlier (i.e. in May 2003, when the Shian site was revealed).

Upgrading stature of the nuclear weapons production department of the Ministry of Defense

In February 2008, new changes in the organizational structure of the Mojdeh site were reported. According to the Iranian opposition, Tehran had moved its nuclear projects into a new phase and established for the first time a command and control center to complete the bomb-making project. This new entity, Advanced Technology Application Development Center, was established and expanded in the same location, the Mojdeh site. This was an independent body of the Ministry of Defense, with its own departments and sub-divisions.

New changes in Mojdeh to cover up its activities

In September 2009, Tehran suspended the Advanced Technology Application Development Center in order to provide an official and legal cover for its activities at the Mojdeh site. Subsequently, Tehran named the Mojdeh site and Malek Ashtar

University as the Pardis of Malek Ashtar University. "Pardis," is referred to as a 'Technology Park,' and with permission from the Ministry of Science, one was established in every university to produce and present its own research. However, the Pardis at Malek Ashtar went on with its activities without following legal procedures in other Iranian universities, meaning it never sought to be officially registered under the Ministry of Science and Higher Education and was merely intended to function as a cover-up.

As a result, Mojdeh became a branch of Malek Ashtar University, which is itself affiliated with the Defense Ministry. A sign at the entrance gate read: Malek Ashtar University, New Technology Complex. Inside, nuclear activities continued in secret and unabated, while the structures and personnel of the nuclear organization were spread throughout the university.

Mohsen Fakhrizadeh became the head of Pardis in Tehran, i.e. the entity consisting of Mojdeh and the "Pardis" section of Malek Ashtar University.

Organization for New Defense Research: New name for nuclear weapon production organization

In March 2011, the Defense Ministry reorganized this independent organization as the SPND. Under the new structure and hierarchy, SPND reported independently to the Deputy Minister of Defense.

According to reports from inside the regime, obtained by the opposition, in light of the policy that the regime had adopted vis-à-vis the international community, and since it had no intention of responding to IAEA questions or allowing inspection of suspicious military centers, it saw no need for maintaining the previous structural organization and once again consolidated and restructured its nuclear activities within an independent entity.

This reorganization was based on a review of the entity's new activities in 2010, and it had been restructured with the objective of accelerating its work and facilitating its efforts by providing more concentration of the activities. Under the new organization, the capabilities and offices of some sections of Malek Ashtar University were placed at the service of the new organization to carry out research and production requested by it.

Mohsen Fakhrizadeh continued to head this organization. He relinquished his previous positions and was no longer the "President of Pardis of Malek Ashtar University in Tehran" or the deputy dean of this university. The headquarters of SPND remained at the Mojdeh site, adjacent to Malek Ashtar University. The office of Mohsen Fakhrizadeh was transferred from Malek Ashtar University to the Mojdeh site.

Tight security and counter-intelligence regulations and measures are imposed on SPND personnel.

Relocation of SPND Command Center

In October 2013, the new address of the SPND command center was Tehran, Pasdaran Avenue, Sanay-e (Lakpour) Avenue, south side (across from Chamran Hospital).

In order to remove all traces and deceive the IAEA inspectors in the course of possible inspections, SPND's activities were divided into two sections. Each division had its own separate location.

The sensitive and covert portion, the existence of which demonstrates the military dimensions of the regime's nuclear program, was relocated to the new address.

The non-sensitive section was deliberately kept at the former site so that in the event of inspections, the agency would not be greeted with vacant premises that would lead them to conclude that a relocation of activities had taken place.

The transfer of SPND that started in late 2013 was completed in 2014. The offices of Dr. Mohsen Foroughizadeh, head of the SPND New Technologies Division, which is focused on nuclear physics, were among those transferred to the new location.

Mohsen Fakhrizadeh, a Brigadier General of the IRGC, is still the director of SPND. He is the key person in the military dimensions of the Iranian nuclear program. The IAEA has sought to interview him for years to no avail.

The report provided by the opposition in October 2014 points out that Fakhrizadeh's office is located at the Beheshti complex at Iran Electronics Industries (Farsi acronym: SAIRAN). SAIRAN is the electronic department of the Defense Ministry and is located at Pasdaran Avenue, Moghan Street.

Due to the fact that the information filed and kept at Fakhrizadeh's office is highly sensitive, the whereabouts of the office have been hidden even from the heads of the various departments of SAIRAN.

Issue of PMD and nuclear negotiations between Iran and P5+1

The resolution of PMD issues was an essential and integral part of the negotiations between the Iranian regime and P5+1 on the Iranian nuclear issue that concluded with the Joint Comprehensive Plan of Action (JCPOA). Eventually, it was agreed that the IAEA would provide a report on the PMD and outstanding issues.

The IAEA Director-General Yukiya Amano prepared his report in December 2016 and presented it to the IAEA board.

The 16-page report examined each and every one of the outstanding issues and the extent to which they were answered during the past several months of exchanges with the Iranian regime.

The report said the investigation did not answer all outstanding questions about Iran's past research but concluded that Iran had conducted weapons' research as recently as 2009.

Over the years, the regime has incessantly and systematically worked to destroy any document or evidence about its clandestine activities to build the nuclear bomb. Yet the IAEA's conclusion countered years of Iranian claims that its nuclear program was for peaceful purposes and the claim that the Iranian supreme leader had issued a fatwa (religious decree) against the development of nuclear weapons.

The report stated: "The Agency assesses that, before the end of 2003, an organizational structure was in place in Iran suitable for the coordination of a range of activities relevant to the development of a nuclear explosive device. Although some activities took place after 2003, they were not part of a coordinated effort" and specified that the regime's activities have continued at least until 2009.

"The Agency has no credible indications of activities in Iran relevant to the development of a nuclear explosive device after 2009."

The year 2003, that was referred to as the turning point in the regime's attempts to obtain a nuclear bomb, pertained to the disclosure of the Lavizan-Shian site by the NCRI in May 2003.

Despite all the hampering and lack of cooperation by Tehran the report brushed aside the regime's deceptions, including its falsifications regarding the exploding bridge wire (EBW) or the multipoint initiator (MPI). Accordingly, explanations offered by the regime in this regard have at times been contradictory or inconsistent. The report underscores that EBW detonators developed by Iran "have characteristics relevant to a nuclear explosive device" and that "the MPI technology developed by Iran has characteristics relevant to a nuclear explosive device."

As for the Parchin military installation, where the Iranians prepared an "explosives firing chamber" in 2000, the IAEA rejected Tehran's explanations that the site has been used "for the storage of chemical material for the production of explosives."

While emphasizing that "extensive activities" undertaken by Iran at this installation in recent years, including destruction of buildings and landscaping, "seriously undermined" the agency's ability to determine what existed there before, the report said "Information available to the Agency in relation to hydrodynamic testing indicated that Iran made and installed a large cylinder at the Parchin military complex in 2000. Other information indicated that this cylinder matched the parameters of an explosive firing chamber featured in publications of the foreign experts. The information available to the Agency, including the results of the analysis of the samples and the satellite images, does not support Iran's statements on the purpose of the building."

Despite IAEA report, scores of questions remain unanswered, many places unchecked

The IAEA report clearly indicated a lack of cooperation on the part of the regime with the Agency and was far from being conclusive.

While it actually left many questions unanswered, the report clearly affirmed that the IAEA had been barred from direct access to military sites, as well as the opportunity to interview key experts and individuals relevant to the nuclear weapons program of Iran, among other obstructions.

Over the years of the IAEA investigations, Tehran never provided unfettered and timely access to disputed sites. On many occasions trails of face lifting and major changes in disputed sites were evident even after long delayed access was provided to IAEA inspectors who could observe the changes that had been made.

Had the international stakeholders adopted a firm stance regarding the illegal actions of this regime, surely further dimensions of this program would have been exposed and the Agency could have disclosed many more cases of regime's attempts to obtain the nuclear bomb.

In the meantime, the Iranian opposition once more exposed on December 1, 2016 that even concurrent with the IAEA investigations to prepare the report, the Iranian regime had set up a top-secret committee to draft the responses to the demands and queries of the IAEA. According to the Iranian opposition, the secret committee was comprised of top officials from the IRGC and Ministry of Defense Armed Forces Logistics, whose task was to cover up the potential military dimensions of the ongoing Iranian nuclear program.

According to the Iranian opposition, the committee was actively forging suitable scenarios for non-military usage of the nuclear program, which would seem plausible to the IAEA, and to falsely convince the international community that Iran has never been after the nuclear bomb. This same committee prepared the PMD answers delivered to the IAEA on August 15, 2015.

Given the familiarity of this committee with the military aspects of the nuclear program, it was tasked to draft the necessary scenarios about the non-military usage of the program to cover up regime's objective to obtain the nuclear bomb. Mohsen Fakhrizadeh, the key individual in the regime's nuclear weapons program who is a member of this committee, finalized the responses and handed them down to the "safeguards section" of the AEOI, which is the entity that presents Iran's official responses to the international inspectors to be passed along to the IAEA.

With the passage of time and Tehran's repeated ballistic missile tests since the implementation of the JCPOA, and growing concerns regarding the capability of these missiles to carry nuclear warheads, it has become more evident that the Agency must continue its investigation into the military dimensions of Iran' nuclear program and demand a detailed and complete response to the true nature of the Iranian regime's program.

Military dimensions of the Iranian regime's nuclear program remain at the core of the concern regarding the nature and purpose of the program. Access to all Iranian sites as well as o the regime's experts and documents must be sought even more vigorously by the IAEA.

Former Vice-President of the European Parliament, Alejo Vidal-Quadras is a professor of nuclear physics and President of the International Committee in Search of Justice (ISJ), a non-governmental organization based in Brussels.

Revolutionary Guards: A terrorist force?

Yves Bonnet

Something that dictatorships all have in common is an obsession with their own longevity. Nothing is more important to them than to put in place the instruments to ensure their survival, which have virtually the same characteristics, barring minor differences: fanatical devotion to the regime, iron discipline within the police services, and ferocity in the repression of opposition "plots", both at home and abroad, even going so far as to commission terrorist acts on foreign territory. Some of the so-called security services have pushed the limits of barbarity to genocide and crimes against humanity.

We have long believed that the paroxysm of brutality had been reached with the Nazi and Fascist regimes. The victors of the Second World War, led by the United States of America, did not adopt the mistaken policies of the first international institutions such as the League of Nations, which sought to maintain peace without establishing instruments to do so; instead, the ambitious and praiseworthy plan of the victors was to organize not only *coexistence* but *cooperation* between nations. Democracy became de facto the primary reference of the new States. After the victory of the free governments over the dictatorships, republics came into existence all over the world, certainly differing from one to another, but with identical objectives: elections and freedom.

Nevertheless, the rightness of the words could not disguise very different situations, even opposing situations, and dictatorships gained a legitimized place without actually being legitimate. In New York, the seat of the United Nations, an organization under the domination of the five self-proclaimed victors of the war, it became habitual to intervene in conflicts between nations or even within nations – not necessarily with armed troops – if it was shown that principles such as the right of people to freedom were not respected. On paper, military interventions on foreign soil were condemned, the most striking and shocking example being colonial wars. However, with the help of semantic creativity the legal obstacle was overcome in two stages. First it was considered sufficient argument to intervene at the request of one of the countries, without studying the real justification, which was the case in the Korean War, and in Vietnam, or when Warsaw Pact troops intervened periodically to quell domestic revolts in Hungary, Czechoslovakia and East Germany. Then there was legal ineptitude, the invocation of the *Right of Humanitarian Intervention*, which was used to justify characterized attacks against constituted States, going as far as their destruction or dismantling.

The dictatorships followed another track, that of showing their respect for human rights and freedoms through State terrorism. They use different forms of oppression that should be recognized individually, even if they all have the same end purpose: the perpetuation of the system.

The first, internal repression, is a survival obligation. The autocrats know that they're governing against the will of the people, so their goal is constraint. It's a question of suppressing the threat the people will pose if they recover the use of their sovereignty. So it's essential – vital – to stop that. Popular sovereignty arises from two sources: there are public freedoms – the right to choose their representatives and to supervise their action, which includes the right of alternation of government, so as to punish improper or inappropriate conduct; then there is what the English-speaking world calls *habeas corpus*, which comprises a number of freedoms the most emblematic of which is the freedom of opinion and expression – in plain language, the freedom of the press. This body of rights represents the essence of democracy, regardless of the institutional framework within which it exists. This may be a hereditary monarchy as in the northern European countries or an elected government, as in the European countries having been *part of the Roman Empire*.

Dictatorships, on the other hand, refuse to submit to the will of the people, and impose their own. Since the appropriation of power is totally arbitrary, its principle cannot be argued, and therein lies the entire problem of their legitimization. The first autocrats chose the simplest argument, from empirical experience, such as can be seen on the playground and in prison: *force*. Thereafter, there was significant progress; for centuries, absolute monarchies became self-perpetuating by advancing an uncertain right, a legitimacy that could be delegated by a temporal or spiritual force – God, in this case. *Divine right* was born. It has used all religions to give it cover and, of course, the best and often the only argument: force. Challenged in the eighteenth century by French philosophers, and overthrown in the Revolution, divine right gave way to *sovereignty of the people*, which has since become the sole incontestable source of legitimacy.

Nevertheless, the temptation of totalitarian rule is rising again, but, since one has to adapt to the times, it is clad in concessions, such as: universal suffrage, which can always be cheated; the appointment of representatives, which can be directed; or even relative freedom of the press, which is easy to manipulate. But the alternation of power – the key element of democracy – is missing. Because of this, the withholding of freedoms and the violation of human rights become obligatory for a totalitarian government, which has to ceaselessly dissuade those who oppose it, and it can never slacken the pressure or else it will be overthrown. One observation is not new. Montesquieu writes *"We see clearly that a despotic government needs no censors."* And the author of *"l'Esprit des Lois"* (The Spirit of the Laws) explains that *"... fear is the (guiding) principle of the despotic government. There is neither honor nor virtue in a despotic government."* Those who may be astonished by the premonition of the greatest of the French political thinkers should remember that the same is true of the nature of mankind.

A despotic government must inspire fear, or it will be overthrown. It can use any means available, especially as there is no legal impediment to their use. In our own times, power has much more compelling arguments than the despots of the eighteenth century. It can call on professional terrorists, which they could not. Crowd manipulation techniques and *violation by political manipulation* have become rife, as Sergei Chakhotin demonstrated. Despotic governments can present powerful arguments by means of propaganda, particularly if they can rely on the argument of force as the last resort: they persuade with words and mass demonstrations and, if that fails, they impose their will.

The use of force is the last resort, and differing degrees of intensity can be used, varying from dissuasion to *terrorization*. The Franco dictatorship in Spain, however intolerable it may have seemed to the Spanish people, had to hide behind the reassuring appearance of a country welcoming tourists while, in General Jorge Videla's Argentina, the regime could engage in summary killings, throwing prisoners into the sea from helicopters, to a resounding silence from the media and from governments worldwide. We are amused at the ridiculous behavior of the atrocious Kim Jong Un, a privileged ally of the Islamic Republic of Iran. The popular French proverb *"Qui se ressemble s'assemble"* (those who are alike converge together) has never been so true as when applied to this relationship, which isn't one of mere chance.

In Iran hangings and public floggings occur almost daily; the regime uses these macabre demonstrations to discourage any form of opposition. This is terrorization, and we have reached the ultimate phase of constraint, which is *State terrorism*, which justifies considering *any violent act targeting the civil population – and, additionally, the State that ordered it and the people or groups of people that carried it out – to be befitting of the adjective "terrorist".*

External repression is another weapon of constraint in a dictatorship's armory. In every case – and, luckily, there are but few – absolute ferocity has been used against opponents, who leave the country, obviously, for safety reasons but equally to spread their message. This diaspora is largely made up of intellectuals, who can adapt more easily, and who can make a significant contribution to the cause they support and to which they are devoted. These exiles are not impressed by the arguments advanced by the regimes they fight, and there are few defections from their ranks. They represent a real threat to the authorities at home, because they find convincing arguments to attract people from all spheres to their cause, who are concerned about the spread of terrorism worldwide. Logically, they are priority targets for the political police, who are judged entirely on their results.

Actions carried out by the political police in foreign countries, are both crimes in the Penal Code and violations of international law. The most striking examples, because they are the most persistent, are gathered from VEVAK (MOIS), the Iranian Ministry of Intelligence and Security, which from its inception has engaged in numerous violent operations to assassinate the regime's opponents. The examples of former Prime Minister Shapour Bakhtiar, beheaded with a knife, or of Kazem Rajavi, a pure intellectual, are tragic illustrations of the widespread commissioning of acts that are also an attack on the sovereignty of the countries in which they take place. The dimension of the crimes and their end purpose enables them to be classified as terrorist acts; *this justifies considering any act designed to export violence to the territory of foreign States as befitting of the definition "terrorist".*

Working from this dual nature of a terrorist act – repressive when perpetrated domestically, and criminal when carried out abroad, it is possible to build up a pen portrait of the terrorist State. Clearly, it is a state which will not be deterred from any crime to ensure its continuance, and which plainly falls within the definition by the jurist François de Menthon, prosecutor at the Nuremburg trials, in 1945 of a crime against humanity: *a crime against human laws, motivated by an ideology that is a crime against the spirit, returning humanity to barbarism.*

Truth to tell, few countries resort to the whole range of terrorist acts to ensure their longevity. Some, indeed most, settle for internal repression, which might go as far as a crime against humanity; they do not risk defying the countries that shelter their opponents. Others make hunting their opponents internationally a key part of their security policy. The first category includes nations that are sensitive about publicity, and that can't risk appearing disrespectful of international law. A simple threat of being blacklisted as a terrorist state is sufficient to dissuade them. Among the second are a minority of governments that prefer to settle their accounts outside their own national territory, and that often resort to intermediaries, as the Lebanese Hezbollah or Ahmed Djibrill's PFLP. There are few that resort to every form of criminal activity, and, though they fall short of being absolute terrorists, are still absolutely terrorists.

The community of nations which should be the major regulator of terrorist activity is not fulfilling its role. In fact, far from warning or condemning those of its members that infringe human rights and international law, it instead shows extreme severity against organizations to which the status of a resistance movement cannot be applied precisely because it doesn't exist. The failure to recognize the right to resist and the right to insurrection is a flagrant omission; the French declaration of human rights of 1793 addressed it and was ratified by referendum.

It is as if the international community was concerned only with the perpetuity of nations, regardless of their nature. The packaging and labeling are enough – no need to open the box to check the contents.

This universal blindness is explained by the simple weight of diplomatic conventions, which distort the judgement of professional diplomats and politicians. As long as it is easy for a State to request and obtain a condemnation of an opposition organization without any trial, the converse sanction applied to State police institutions will have no chance of succeeding.

In the recent past the political police of the Warsaw Pact countries, or those of the dictatorial regimes of Latin America, aided by the United States, have slipped through the net and their brutalities set aside, if not tolerated, by democratic countries. A case can be made for or against designating the Kurdistan Workers Party (PKK), the Popular Front for the Liberation of Palestine (PFLP), the Irish Republican Army (IRA) or the Ulster Volunteer Force (UVF) as terrorist organizations, but no file is ever opened for assassinations or kidnapping committed against them by Interpol's member institutions.

This dichotomy should not exist when democracies present their model as **the** universal reference. Terror attacks against national opponents can be explained away, if necessary, by the temporary or fortuitous nature of the breaches of national and international law. But this becomes complicity when *homicidal* acts are committed repeatedly and continually. We can therefore regard the French SDECE, the British MI6 or the Spanish CNP as having committed violent acts or even murders (modestly described as *"Omo operations"* in France) against persons or organizations threatening the internal security of the State, and then subsequently reverting to a respect for the democratic law. This is quite different from the actions of political or military police institutions such as those that carried out acts of brutality in

General Videla's Argentina, in General Pinochet's Chile, in Cuba under the Castro regime, or in the Greece of the colonels. These examples of continuous repression that are inherent to their regimes indisputably qualify them as terrorists. However, they are outstripped in terms of both efficiency and duration by the example shown to us daily by a great nation that is one of the greatest in historical terms, one of the richest humanly speaking, not to say one of the most promising and, in any event, one of the pillars of the Orient.

Iran, which is incorrect in calling itself an *Islamic Republic*, presents the characteristic of a perfect absolutist political structure because it concentrates all its constitutional, executive, legislative and judicial powers in a single pair of hands, and it commits the task of ensuring the survival of the regime by any means, including terrorism, to an all-powerful repressive body. This institution is sub-divided into a *conventional* intelligence service and security service, the Ministry of Intelligence (VEVAK) and an elite corps, the Islamic Revolutionary Guard Corps (IRGC), a military body of the kind one thought had disappeared forever with Hitler's SA and SS.

In 2009, I wrote a book about the former of these, entitled *Vevak, au service des ayatollahs: Histoire des services secrets iraniens [Vevak, at the Service of the Ayatollahs – The History of the Iranian Secret Services]*. For the Revolutionary Guards, readers can refer to the excellent work published by Mehdi Abrishamchi, a leading member of the opposition, in 2008. If you study these two Iranian power structures, you can judge the globality and the consistency of a security policy that it is difficult to qualify other than as terrorist.

A recent report by two NGOs, the International Committee In Search of Justice (ISJ), and the European-Iraqi Freedom Association (EIFA), on the "Destructive role of Iran's Islamic Revolutionary Guard Corps (IRGC) in the Middle East" supports this description.

The Islamic Revolutionary Guard Corps was founded in May 1979, only three months after the coming to power of the Islamic regime in Iran. The name and title of this body makes no reference to "Iran", because its mandate goes far beyond the geographic limits of Iran. It is the main instrument of the religious Supreme Leader (*Velayat-e faqih*) for the mission of establishing an "Islamic Caliphate".

Brigadier General Ahmad Gholampour, formerly head of the IRGC, mentioned this in an interview with Fars, an official Iranian press agency: "The [regular] Army's mission is to protect Iran's geographic frontiers. But the word 'Iran' doesn't feature in the title of the IRGC. That means that it seeks to defend the Islamic revolution and its acquisitions, regardless of geographic frontiers… It is the duty of the IRGC to intervene in any place where it detects or feels there is a danger to the Revolution. We have a free hand to involve ourselves in any geographic area, and in any area of political, social or cultural life."

The Revolutionary Guards, or *Pasdaran,* are the armed branch of the clerical regime, and differ from the Ministry of Intelligence in two respects.

The first aspect is its **institutionalization**. The IRGC is an integral part of the State's apparatus, and two articles of the Constitution declare it to be so.

In the first place, it is the subject of *Principle* (or Article) 150, which establishes its founding "in the first days of the victory of the revolution", and perpetuates its existence on the same terms as the Army. The appointment of its head by the Supreme Leader is provided for in Principle 110, Article 6, paragraph e, in the same way as for the principal dignitaries of the regime. The *pasdaran* are tasked with the mission of supervising the regime's nuclear activities as proof of the confidence that the State machine places in them.

Article 1 of the IRGC's Articles, written in 1979, specifies: "The IRGC is an institution under the supreme command of the Head of State, and its object is to protect Iran's Islamic Revolution and the acquisitions therefrom, and to work continually to accomplish the divine ideals and extend the sovereignty of divine law on the basis of the laws of the Islamic Republic of Iran, strengthening the Islamic Republic's defensive structure with the cooperation of other armed forces, military formations and popular forces."

Article 11 of the same text relates to the training of its personnel: "The training of members of the IRGC will be based on the directives of the *Velayat-e faqih* in the ideological, political and military domains, in order to attain the skills and capacity needed to accomplish the missions with which they are tasked." Article 47 states: "With regard to political or ideological questions the IRGC is controlled by the *Velayat-e faqih*."

The second original characteristic of the IRGC lies in its vocation as a **means of destabilization**; it is qualified to operate outside Iran for conventional missions (murders and terror attacks), and to take on a training mission for every terrorist movement in the world, taking over a function which we believed had disappeared with the overthrow or weakening of the lay Arab republics, Syria, Iraq, and Libya, and that Pakistan had also carried out to the great benefit of Al Qaida and Islamism, under American monitoring.

Iran is interesting, both because of the cosmopolitan character of its inhabitants and the doctrinal development of its teachings. In fact (and the nuance is important), while the Arab nations we have just named see their action of training (and arming) as *identity terrorism* linked with the Palestinian peoples' struggle for the recognition of their rights (these camps disappeared one after another during the 1980s), the CIA in Pakistan, with jihadist assistance, followed by the Islamic Revolutionary Guard Corps in Iran, made the promotion of *messianic terrorism* one of their prime goals; for the latter, it would be the militarized arm of the conquest of the Ummah.

Thus charged with one of the regime's two essential missions, which we should remember, are first, *to survive and grow stronger*, which is entrusted to the VEVAK, and to *export the Islamist revolution*, which naturally falls to it, the Revolutionary Guards have adopted a military structure. The IRGC has five branches: the land army, the air force (mainly armed with missiles and drones), the navy, the *Bassij* resistance force and the Quds Force.

The Bassij (*or Mobilization*) was formed in November 1979, when "students" – among them the future President of the Republic, Mahmoud Ahmadinejad, and the future Vice-President Responsible for the Environment, Masoumeh Ebtekar – overran the United States Embassy in Tehran. Consecrated by Khomeini, integrated into the corps of *pasdaran* and then confirmed by Khamenei, this organization – which it would be incorrect to consider as having taken form spontaneously – has gradually become the regime's permanent domestic repression force. It is both the complement and a *concealed extension* of the IRGC – the command structure of the IRGC – that provides it with additional personnel when necessary, and enables it to stay out of the limelight with regard to the regime's domestic policing.

The Bassij has both an everyday operational role, and a contingency role.

In everyday life, *bassijis* are supposed to *promote virtue and prohibit vice* – hollow words, characteristic of the morality police. This means that the young people who enroll in the Bassij in their district **make** the law and claim **to be** the law. In a desperately poor country where the authorities show their contempt for human dignity, they become the district bullyboys and Khamenei grants them wide-ranging rights, varying from entry into any suspect premises – including homes – to rights of inspection and of arrest, as well as control over national and international flights.

They are paid part-time only – which is nevertheless a privilege in a country burdened with a structural economic crisis – but they are not particularly efficient. What makes them formidable is the tightly-meshed networking of the districts, and good knowledge of their territory. *Bassijis* are intolerant and fanatical, and they inspire fear. In order to build their image of ferocity, the regime over-states their numbers, and the 321 000 quoted by Mehdi Abrishamchi in his book has risen to an incredible 8 million, without possibility of contradiction. This manipulation is anything but innocent. It aims to instill a permanent feeling of insecurity among the population. *Bassijis* maintain the climate of fear, which is advantageous to the clerics, just like the Hitler youth did when they harassed Jews, communists and socialists sixty years earlier. Their ability to enter private property at will, which leaves a lot of room for settling scores, can be a deterrent, particularly among student circles where people are naturally given to protest.

The two structures we have described above are complementary, and they intermingle, with the Bassij enabling the IRGC to stay in the background of incidents in the streets, although they are commanded by IRGC officers. This works by means of a dual membership, which facilitates the integration of *Bassiji* reinforcements into IRGC personnel, if needed. This bivalence occurs above all in the higher levels of the hierarchy, in the towns and geographical departments, where *Bassij* leaders are frequently middle-rank Revolutionary Guards. This point is only important insofar as those in power pride themselves on being able immediately to triple the IRGC's strength by using *Bassijis*, whereas many of the new combatants are already included in the mobilizable personnel. In any case, *Bassijis* receive ongoing military training, which extends as far as the handling of heavy infantry weapons, and the finance is not stymied. During the war with Iraq they were a reserve which could be tapped to fill the enormous losses suffered by the Iranian forces, notably the IRGC.

The *Bassij* was to learn a great deal during the revolution, and would contribute to turning its course. As is written in the Islamic Constitution, *Bassijis* intervened very early to contain demonstrations, mostly by the democratic opposition, and to make sure that the religious authorities had the last word on the street. On the opposing side, the People's Mojahedin Organization of Iran (PMOI or MEK) would also learn very quickly: they didn't intend to allow the Islamists to take over a revolution which was *against the Shah* but *not in favor of the Islamists*. In spite of the Imperial regime's heavy losses among the PMOI's higher ranks, they managed – unlike the mullahs – to attract increasingly large crowds. They went as far as presenting a large show of force on June 20, 1981, with half a million people on the streets of the capital. The regime found this huge demonstration disturbing and put it down bloodily, and the women and men who had banked on a liberalization of the government went clandestine.

Thus engaged in the maintenance of Islamic order, the *Bassijis* were increasingly at the forefront in the repression of demonstrations .Things had taken an irreversible turn towards violence. But the theocracy knew that it could count on a repressive force that was capable of breaking up the inevitable riots. The popular uprisings of the 1990s, and the student movement in July 1999 following the banning of the newspaper, *Salam*, were demonstrations of the ferocity of their action, before the peak of their brutality was unleashed during the disturbances of July 2009, which resulted in an incontestable record of over 150 dead and thousands arrested, imprisoned, tortured and even raped.

Bassijis received the greatest blame. Their involvement in the regime's reign of terror could no longer escape scrutiny. However, the regime went too far in its political manipulations and, in backing Mahmoud Ahmadinejad for the Presidential election of 2009, it crossed the yellow line of internal consensus among various internal factions, which was more personal than doctrinal, and finally found itself facing a circumstantially-formed majority that included certain elements of the conservative factions. The Supreme Leader had no choice other than to call in the *Bassijis* yet again, to restore order.

The truth is undeniable: through the *Bassijis*, the IRGC is, together with VEVAK, a proven political institution for maintaining order, and its methods reveal it to be an instrument of terror. We shall see later under what conditions it could be challenged in the international courts, which are now better prepared to deal with such an issue since the creation of an International Criminal Court by the Treaty of Rome.

The IRGC therefore has a powerful arm in the *Bassij*, which suppresses or tries to suppress popular discontent, which is ever rising. The IRGC can also call on another arm, this time to press the regime's interests in countries in the process of being conquered or brought under the regime's influence. This second arm is the *Quds Force*, which came to prominence during its fighting in the Syrian conflict but which, in fact, had already been operational in other geographical contexts, in Syria, Lebanon, Palestine and Yemen, either directly or via a proxy, all linked to the Iranian Republic's expansionist and messianic policies.

The Quds [or Jerusalem] Force (IRGC-QF) was formed in 1990, after the death of the first Supreme Leader, Ayatollah Ruhollah Khomeini. Described in powerful circles as "the genesis of an international Islamic army", this terrorist organization has spread through the region like a cancer. Today, the IRGC has affiliate terrorist networks in at least twelve countries in the region. The terrorist activities have affected thirteen countries. According to the US Department of State, "The IRGC-QF is the regime's primary mechanism for cultivating and supporting terrorists abroad." It acts through a multitude of auxiliaries like the Badr Brigade. The IRGC formed this force from Iraqi prisoners-of-war during the Iran-Iraq conflict and inserted them into Iraqi territory, taking advantage of the US invasion of 2003, organized into four divisions and two brigades under the command of the Quds Force.

The Badr fought openly against the American occupation forces in Iraq, and hunted down former officers in Saddam Hussein's army – mostly Sunnis. Unlike the foreign militias such as the Badr, the Quds Force has no established military unit, division or battalion. It is a framework within which formations of Revolutionary Guards evolve and operate. For example, in Syria units identified as Quds Force are actually IRGC brigades – the Fajr Brigade based in Shiraz and units recruited from other IRGC divisions. Groups of foreign mercenaries are added under arrangements that we will look at later.

The Quds Force acts as a clearing house, gathering and running organizations of different nationalities or origins, which undertake violent overseas operations, ranging from combat – like a kind of Foreign Legion – to organized crime, which places them in the terrorist category. The associated units identified are the Lebanese Hezbollah, the Iraqi Badr Brigade, the Iraqi Asa'ib Ahl al-Haq and the Iraqi Kata'ib Hezbollah. A common factor in these units is that they are exclusively Shiite, which makes coordination easier.

In Iraq, paramilitary groups affiliated to the IRGC are involved in terrorism and in crimes against humanity. In 2009, the United States Department of State qualified the Kata'ib Hezbollah as a Foreign Terrorist Organization and accused the group of attacks against American forces. Its leader, known as Abu Mahdi Al-Muhandis, began working with the IRGC in Kuwait in the 1980s and was responsible for the attack on the United States Embassy in that country. At present, the group is under the direct command of the Quds Force commander, Qassem Soleimani.

Another terrorist group under the auspices of the IRGC's Quds Force is Asa'ib Ahl al-Haq. According to the US Army, the group's commander, Sheikh Qais al-Khazali, has supervised terrorist operations including an attack in Karbala in 2007 in which five US soldiers were killed. Al-Khazali is also thought to have organized the kidnapping of five British citizens in Iraq in 2007.

Nowadays these paramilitaries identify themselves as the "Popular Mobilization Forces" and are commanded directly by the IRGC, which supplies them with equipment, arms, intelligence and artillery support. The "Popular Mobilization Forces" (Al-Hashd Al-Sha'abi) – which is now an official armed force of the Iraqi state – fills in for the weaknesses of the Iraqi Army. However, it is controlled by the IRGC, represented by such veterans of terrorism as Abu Mahdi Al-Muhandis and Hadi Ameri (the historic leader of the Badr). Both have dual nationality – Iraqi and Iranian.

On July 26, 2015, the state-affiliated Iranian press agency Fars published a report underlining the role of the latter in starting up the "Popular Mobilization Forces":

"Abu Mahdi Al-Muhandis, whose real name is Jamal Jafaar Ibrahimi, is officially the joint commander-in-chief of the "Popular Mobilization Force". This Quds officer is one of the seventeen individuals accused of involvement in the attacks on the United States Embassy and the French Embassy in Kuwait in 1983 and in the attempted assassination of the Emir Jaber Al-Ahmad Al-Sabah of Kuwait in 1985. He is also accused of being involved in the hijacking of a Kuwaiti Airlines aircraft in 1984. Al-Muhandis is also one of the brains behind Ibrahim Jaafari and Nouri Maliki, both of whom became Prime Ministers."

In an interview with the Lebanese daily Al Akhbar, Al-Muhandis stated, "If it were not for the extensive support of the Islamic Republic and, above all, the personal support of Ayatollah Khamenei, the creation of this organization ['Popular Mobilization Forces'] would have been fundamentally impossible, especially if we take into account all the measures taken in this respect. Khamenei ordered our brothers in the IRGC to support the 'Popular Mobilization Forces,' and the IRGC supplied us with arms and munitions, as well as advice and planning of military operations."

"Imad Mughniyeh and Mustafa Badreddine, successively heads of the Lebanese Hezbollah military organization, both played a fundamental part in the organization of Iraqi resistance against the Americans," according to al-Muhandis. Al-Muhandis' admissions tell us a lot about the Islamic Republic's intentions in Iraq. He states that "We will send units (from Hashd Al-Sha'abi) throughout the whole region if necessary, wherever Iraq's security is threatened."

A new terrorist military group set up by the IRGC in Iraq is Saraya Al Khorasani. The group says that it was founded by Hamid Taqavi, one of the principle figures in the Quds Force in Iraq. He was killed in December 2014 at the front in Samarra.

"In the years following the American occupation of Iraq, Iranian IEDs (improvised explosive devices) targeting American tanks and armored vehicles were activated by Hajji Hamid (Taqavi)," says a member of Badr in October 2015 named Sadeq al-Moussavi. He added in his Facebook page, "All the Iraqi groups got high-quality advice, assistance and arms, which this man supplied them. He never left Iraq during the occupation, except for a few weeks, or for other attacks that he intended to mount in Palestine, Lebanon or Yemen."

From the year 2000 on, and in the wide area open in the Middle East to American intervention, the Quds Force saw the opening of two fields of wide experimentation that both turned into battlefields. They were Iraq and Syria. It was a cruel historical revenge on these two countries in quest of modernity, and initially inspired by the same progressive lay ideology, that of *the Ba'ath*, to be under a brutal dictatorship of a foreign nation that was itself under an ochlo-theocracy. Of the two vanished dictators, Saddam Hussein, certainly the most convincing and the most anxious for the economic and social progress of his people, was cynically sacrificed by the United States and its coalition; the second, Hafez Assad, shamelessly established the succession for his descendants like any ordinary monarch and, having betraying the master of Baghdad, he then betrayed Syria by reneging on the initial political ideals at the time of his accession to power.

This was a double victory for Iran and promised expansion, of which the Quds Force is now becoming the instrument. It moved into Iraq and got involved in Syria, supporting the Shiite faction of the population in each country, notwithstanding the risk of destabilizing the society in the countries and becoming the objective ally of certain American and Israeli spheres, with their *"Great Middle East"* constitution initiative, by which the current States would be replaced by a handful of small entities based on religion or race, and thus rendered less dangerous. This shortsighted strategy is the contrary of a search for the indispensable political compromise involving Jews, Muslims and Christians, followed by a commitment to regional growth – which, furthermore, is inevitable with the discovery of petrochemicals in the Eastern Mediterranean.

Iran cannot look on this fragmentation with an unfavorable eye, given that the Shiism of which it has appointed itself the standard bearer is a minority religion in the East. However, it can expect a lot from the small States that will be dependent on its subsidies, its oil or its military strength. This is especially true if it had nuclear weapons.

From 2003 to 2009 the Iranian government resorted to various measures aimed at extending its influence in Iraq. They included terrorist attacks against coalition forces, the assassination of Sunni political figures and demonstrators, and promoting Shiite groups linked with Tehran.

In addition to Shiite groups, Tehran also gave financial support, arms and logistics support to various Sunni groups. The Al-Qaeda's top men in Iran cooperated fully with the Iranian regime, and Al-Qaeda's leader in Iraq, Abu Musab al-Zarqawi, visited Iran, commuting between Iran and Iraq in coordination with the Iranian regime. Later Zarqawi assembled a group of individuals who would form the Islamic State in Iraq and the Near East.

Islamic State (Daesh or ISIS) is a byproduct of the repression of the Iraqi people, notably the Sunnis, under the government of the former Prime Minister Nuri al-Maliki in Iraq and of Bashar Assad in Syria, both of whom were under the influence of Tehran. Paradoxically, the ethnic cleansing of the Sunni population in Iraq contributed to the rise of IS. Neither the Iranian Supreme Leader, nor Maliki, nor Assad could ignore the consequences of their behavior in freeing extremist prisoners from the prisons of Iraq and Syria. Once freed, these extremists considerably swelled the ranks of what would become Islamic State. In November 2014, then-US Secretary of State, John Kerry, told Fox News in an interview that "ISIS was created by Assad releasing 1,500 prisoners from jail and Malaki releasing 1,000 people in Iraq who were put together as a force of terror types." He separately mentioned the Assad regime's purchase of oil produced by ISIS was one of the principal factors that contributed to ISIS's survival. He concluded that Assad and IS had a "symbiotic" relationship.

The IRGC was able to strengthen its interference in Iraq, both politically and militarily, when the American forces left the country.

It was as if the Quds Force was free to hold the strategic line of a declared expansionism. The Shiite paramilitaries it influenced, supported and coordinated acted brutally. They avenged themselves on the former officers of the Iraqi army – a vengeance which the Iraqi Shiites had not even demanded. Men who saw any possibility of keeping their dignity were driven to despair by the Shiite forces, making them the most powerful potential recruits for the Islamic State. Their demands were not publicized, nor was the tenacious persecution of Iranian opposition militants based in the Camp Ashraf and Camp Liberty, leaving dozens dead and hundreds wounded. It is beyond dispute that the terror spread by the hatchet men in the pay of the Quds Force, under Iranian supervision, was much worse than was decried by the Western powers, at a time when insecurity became general, in spite of the burgeoning of foreign private police and generously-paid mercenaries. With no attempt to hide it, General Qassem Soleimani, leader of the Quds Force for over twenty years, became a sort of proconsul whose territory covered that of the formerly-independent states of Iraq and Syria.

The Quds Force, acting as the IRGC's extraterritorial arm, had effectively taken control of the regime's foreign policy through several of its embassies. The regime's embassies in Iraq, Syria, Lebanon, Afghanistan, Yemen, Bahrain and Azerbaijan were all in this category of very special "diplomatic" representations. Even the staff of the Foreign Ministry, who were supposed to take their orders from the Ministry itself, adapted their activities to the will and directives of the IRGC.

In addition to the countries mentioned above, the IRGC had the upper hand in foreign policy in countries such as Armenia, Russia, Turkey, Saudi Arabia, Kuwait, the United Arab Emirates, Qatar and Oman.

The regime's ambassadors in countries like Iraq, Syria and Afghanistan were chosen from the ranks of the Quds Force or people close to the IRGC. This enabled the IRGC to advance its projects by exploiting opportunities offered by the diplomatic immunity of the Embassy and the Ambassador.

Since the invasion of Iraq by the US forces in 2003, Tehran's ambassadors to Iraq had always been chosen from the ranks of the commanders of the Quds Force. The first ambassador to Iraq after the overthrow of the former regime was Brigadier-General Hassan Kazemi Qumi. Before being appointed to Baghdad, he had been

Consul-General in the city of Herat in Afghanistan. In 2011, Brigadier-General Hassan Danaifar replaced Kazemi Qumi. Danaifar had previously been the IRGC's deputy naval commander, and had also commanded the headquarters of the IRGC base at Khatam al-Anbiya.

In January 2017, Brigadier General Iraj Masjedi, director of the Bureau of Iraqi Affairs within the IRGC, and principal advisor to Soleimani, was appointed the Iranian regime's Ambassador to Baghdad. General Masjedi stated, during a ceremony organized for one of the combatants killed in Syria, "In the past, our front line was Anadan, Khorramshahr, Mehran and Haji Omeran (Iranian towns and cities). Today, this frontier has been pushed to Mosul, Lebanon and Aleppo in Syria."

The decisive role of the *Basij* and Quds Force, both emanations from the IRGC, in the durabilization and expansionism of the theocracy, by *military and policing actions*, ought to justify prosecution at the international courts of justice, as per the jurisdiction established during the civil war in Yugoslavia. It must also be stressed that if the Yugoslavian army was legally able to intervene in Croatia and Bosnia, and the Serbian army in Kosovo, Iran's intrusions into neighboring countries cannot be justified in any way.

On what grounds should Iran be condemned for its present role with regard to these two neighboring countries? In the first place, we could speak of their aggression and interference in the internal affairs of another state, similar to when Iran condemned the Americans and the French when they intervened in Lebanon. But no diplomatic service dares.

The creation of the Lebanese Hezbollah was made easier by the IRGC's Liberation Movements Bureau and encouraged by Khomeini in 1981. After his death, Hezbollah vowed allegiance to the political and religious leadership of Ali Khamenei. Following its foundation, all its staff were trained by the IRGC and their salaries were paid by the Quds Force and Khamenei's office.

At the beginning of 1983, the IRGC set up Hezbollah centers in the Bekaa Valley, and openly initiated the training and arming of Hezbollah. Its liaison agent until 1985 was Mohammad Najjar, who later served as Minister of Defense under the presidency of Mahmoud Ahmadinejad. Hezbollah's terrorist operation and those of the Palestinian Islamic Jihad were carried out under the orders and with the support of the IRGC. Deadly terrorist attacks were conducted against American and French civilians in Lebanon between 1983 and 1984. The United States Embassy in Beirut was the target of a suicide attack on April 18, 1983, leaving 63 dead and 120 wounded. Islamic Jihad claimed responsibility a few hours later. The operation was planned by the leaders of the IRGC and guided by IRGC command based in Baalbek and in the Bekaa valley. In 1984, the American Consulate in Beirut was struck by a lorry carrying 500 kilos of explosives. Some twenty people were killed. An extremist group affiliated to the Iranian regime was behind the attack. On October 23, 1983, a lorry carrying 5,543 kilos of TNT crashed into the US Marines' barracks in Beirut. Over 240 US marines were killed. A few minutes later, the French Peace-Keeping Forces Command Headquarters in Beirut was attacked in the same manner, killing 74 people.

At the time, Mohsen Rafiqdoost was the IRGC's commander. He later publicly expressed his pride in the regime's involvement in these terrorist operations. Rafiqdoost's statement was published by the state-run Resalat journal on July 20, 1987: "The US knows that both the TNT and the ideology which in one blast sent to hell 400 officers, NCOs, and soldiers at the Marines headquarters were provided by Iran."

In reality, all the operations mentioned above were carried out by IRGC intelligence agents, with the help of local agents, particularly from IRGC-affiliated Hezbollah forces.

The orders for these terrorist attacks came from the highest level. Hezbollah's budget is paid by Khamenei's personal office, and the Minister of Defense and the regime's Quds Force supply the arms needed by Hezbollah and other Lebanese forces affiliated to the regime. Hezbollah pursues the regime's policies in the region and its forces are currently fighting alongside the IRGC in Syria. The representative of the Quds Force in Lebanon and the liaison officer with Hezbollah is Brigadier-General Zahedi.

In December 2015, the US Treasury imposed financial sanctions on Hezbollah. Thereafter, Hassan Nasrallah, Hezbollah's current General Secretary, admitted his financial dependence on the Iranian regime, declaring that the new series of US sanctions would have no impact on his group, as Hezbollah receives its funding directly from Iran.

Iran could also be condemned for committing crimes against human rights which, when many instances are involved, justify the opening of legal proceedings for crimes against humanity. However, this remains improbable. The established practice is to take action only against states that do not form part of any of the major ensembles that dominate the planet. Therefore, NATO, BRICSAM (of which the members are Brazil, Russia, India, China, South Africa and Mexico) and the SCO (Shanghai Cooperation Organisation, of which the members are China, Russia, Kazakhstan, Kyrgyzstan, Tajikistan, Uzbekistan, India and Pakistan, with Afghanistan, Iran, Mongolia and Belarus as observers, and, finally, Sri Lanka, Turkey, Cambodia, Azerbaijan, Armenia and Nepal as partners in discussions) – which is more than half the world's population – are now *neutralization blocs* within which the application of international sanctions against their members is excluded. What remains possible against African or even European countries without international complicity networks is no longer so for a country which has durable support, in spite of its visible excesses and its contempt for international conventions. Atrocities committed by the Shiite paramilitaries on

Iran's account – in the real sense of the term – will no longer be taken into account when it suits other powers, meaning the majors. By the same logic, the direct intervention by the Revolutionary Guards in the Syrian civil war is occluded by that of Russia, with its commandos and its aircraft, while the Iranian involvement - which is bigger, goes further back in time and has been more constant, being demonstrated by the death in combat of several general officers, and the wounding of their commander-in-chief, Qasem Soleimani. President Assad unarguably owes his continued position at the head of such a ravaged country as much to Iranian as to Russian support.

There remain the abuses committed in Iran itself by the regime's forces of oppression, principally the Basij. Here again, regardless of the degree of inhumanity of Iran's actions against its own nationals, there will never be a majority of countries voting to bring it before the ICC. Getting obstinate about demanding sanctions against Iran because of human rights violations committed by its leaders will serve no purpose while North Korea, and its insane leader, continue to peacefully occupy a seat at the UN and in other international organizations.

However, one measure remains possible, given the number and the variety of consequences that terrorism has in many countries, and given the almost-unanimous condemnation of powerful organizations such as Al-Qaeda and its affiliates, Boko Haram and Islamic State. This measure is the listing of a ministerial or a state organization on the terrorist organizations list. Such a list can be national and, as such, relevant to the authority of a single country, or can be international, like the one the European Union maintains. But one still has to prove Iran's involvement(s) in terrorist activities and their methods.

The VEVAK, or Ministry of Intelligence, has already been the object of sustained attention and sanctioned by the Canadian legal system. The MOIS (VEVAK was given this name by the court) was found guilty by the Federal Court of Appeal, which considered that the MOIS coordinates the assassination of Iranian dissidents, both in and outside Iran, that the MOIS sponsors or directly engages in a varied range of terrorist activities, including the assassination of political dissidents, on a worldwide scale and that the appellant (a certain Ahani, on trial for murder) is effectively a murderer trained by the Iranian secret services. He was also found guilty by the Supreme Court, which confirmed the sentence, stressing that the MOIS sponsors a wide variety of terrorist activities, including the assassination of political dissidents in other countries.

It is not easy to decide between the actions of VEVAK and those that can be attributed to the Quds Force. As in all despotic regimes, the choice between these organizations is made by the supreme authority, or one of its empowered representatives, and the selection criteria are only justified after the event. In the cases that foreign judges (in Iran) have dealt with, the confusion regarding types has been such that requests for international arrest warrants have been filed with bodies such as Interpol, without identifying the departments directly responsible for them. Furthermore, in at least one case – that of the attack on the Jewish Cultural Centre in Buenos Aires – the perpetrator was revealed to be a non-Iranian foreign organization: Lebanese Hezbollah, in fact. The same was true for the attack on the UTA flight in 1989, for which Ahmed Jibril's PFLP was clearly responsible (except in the opinion of Judge Bruguière); Ahmed Jibril presently divides his time between Lebanon and Iran.

In the case of the attack on the Jewish center, the judge, unable to apportion the blame, had to *globalize* it, and asked Interpol to issue international arrest warrants for several Iranian officials, among them Mohsen Rezai (commander-in-chief of the Revolutionary Guards), Ali Fallahian, Minister of Intelligence from 1989 to 1997, General Ahmad Vahidi (commander-in-chief of the Quds Force at the time, and later appointed Minister of Defense),

Ali Akbar Velayati (currently adviser to Iran's Supreme Guide), Ali Akbar Hashemi Rafsanjani (former President of the mullahs' regime), Mohsen Rabbani (former cultural attaché at the Iranian Embassy in Argentina), Ahmad Reza Asghari (former Secretary at the Iranian Embassy in Argentina), and the Lebanese national, Imad Moghniyah, Hezbollah's military commander. Interpol's General Assembly ratified the request by 78 votes to 14, with 26 abstentions. For the department which represents Iran at Interpol, this was a very significant setback.

Ahmad Vahidi, who is still wanted by Interpol for his involvement in the 1994 terrorist attack in Buenos Aires, also took part in the terrorist attack on the Khobar Towers in Saudi Arabia on June 26, 1996.

Within the Quds Force, Saudi Arabian affairs were initially under the jurisdiction of the sixth division of the Persian Gulf. Brigadier-General Ahmad Sharifi, commander of the sixth division, also played a major role in the Khobar Towers explosion. In 1997, when his part in the explosions was revealed, the Quds Force replaced him and then posted him to the Quds University in Qom.

Louis Freeh, former head of the FBI, who went to Saudi Arabia to investigate the terrorist attack, concluded that the Revolutionary Guards were responsible for it. Ten thousand kilos of TNT had been brought in clandestinely in a tanker truck via Lebanon. Nineteen American soldiers were killed and 400 were injured.

More recently, in September 2011, the US government arrested an Iranian national named Manssor Arbabsiar, who was accused of an attempted attack on the Saudi Arabian Ambassador, Adel Jubeir, who is now his country's Foreign Minister. Tehran denied any involvement in the affair.

An eye witness had seen Arbabsiar at the Quds Force headquarters in the Iranian town of Kermanshah on several occasions in 1996 and 1997. The second person involved in this case was his sponsor, Colonel Gholam Shakuri, one of the Quds Force commanders and a member of the Nabi Akram division of Kermanshah province during the Iran-Iraq war.

Up to that time the Iranian regime had rarely been held accountable for its actions, not even before an international court. Three recent developments give encouragement to return to the offensive against one of the most detestable regimes in the world, and to weaken its diplomatic position; two are from Iran and the third is American.

In August 2016, the revelations by the son of Ayatollah Montazeri – who was Khomeini's heir-apparent – about the 1988 massacre in the regime's prisons threw light on the cruelty of those who inspired them, starting with Ayatollah Khomeini himself, and raised the question of starting formal proceedings against those responsible.

Very recently information provided by the Iranian resistance on the existence of Quds Force training camps in Iran justifies at least the opening of an international investigation, which could lead to the organization's inscription on the terrorist organizations list.

Finally, the reversal of America's position regarding Iran, after the position taken by President Donald Trump, is a prompt to the European Union and each of its member states about the execution of the clauses in the July 14, 2015 international agreement regarding the Iran nuclear issue.

Let's look at them again.

The Iranian democratic opposition has forcefully asserted the truth about the 1988 massacre for many years. For a long time, the Iranian lobby has been able to ensure that they were ignored and only appeared in the NCRI's compilation of offenses, which were regarded with reserve if not suspicion. The production of an audio tape by Ayatollah Montazeri's son about his father's warning –

who was then the designated successor to Ruhollah Khomeini – re-opened the whole case, bringing irrefutable proof of the truth of the resistance's accusations, and providing new information. Recently I wrote a full report about the Iranian theocracy's crimes against humanity, with comprehensive coverage of those days of horror, which should not remain unpunished by criminal law.

Even more recently, the social network of the People's Mojahedin Organization of Iran (PMOI) published information, which has been corroborated and verified as usual, about the Quds Force and its involvement in the destabilization of the Near East. The importance of this new information is comparable with that of the revelations by the National Council of Resistance of Iran in 2002 regarding Iran's clandestine nuclear work. It shows the existence of a policy of training of terrorist leaders in various organizations, both Iranian and foreign. Iran has now replaced the Arab states who were accused in the 1970s and 1980s of supporting the Palestinian networks and European terrorist organizations but, unlike Iraq, Syria, Lebanon, in the Bekaa plain, and Libya, which claimed not to be involved in such activities, the clerical State made them a publicized point of its foreign policy, and it is committing its liability, alongside its military resources, in an overall operation aiming at nothing less than its pre-eminence in a world more Arab than Muslim.

While the Shah, who was already expansionist, only aimed to control the north and south shores of the Arabian Gulf, the ochlo-theocracy is looking as far afield as Yemen, Bahrain, Comoros and Afghanistan, and establishing itself in Lebanon by means of Hezbollah, and in Gaza by supporting Hamas. The Shiite religion takes second place in this geopolitical vision. It is actually primarily imperialist, reminiscent of the dreams and the realms of the great Achaemenid emperors, just as Saddam Hussein saw himself as a new Harun al-Rashid. However, in a much more-complicated world, widely penetrated by *barbarian* powers, military might is no longer on the side of the eastern leaders. If

180

Iran wants to control the region, it must resort to trickery, destabilize its enemies, and push them into the vicious circle of oppression and repression – in short, rely on terrorism, the weapon of the weak, to finally become a key player.

The turbulence caused by the American initiatives, first in Afghanistan and then in Lebanon and Palestine and finally in Iraq, are creating the conditions for an upsurgence of terrorism, mutated from an 'identity-driven' terrorism to one with messianic ambitions. To understand its scope, it's enough to look at the contingents of foreign volunteers now entering the Quds Force training centers. Iran has understood that the manipulation of terrorism begins with the training of its officers and even its rank and file. Whoever controls the source can influence the whole network. Whoever controls recruitment can trigger unrest or revolution wherever its own interests so dictate.

It all started around 2012 with the creation of a big so-called training division within the Quds Force. This was seemingly with the assent of the Leader, which gave a new dimension to the policy regarding foreign mercenaries, in both directions. First, it's a question of extending the hunting grounds for volunteers to serve Iranian expansionism. These men are drawn not only from countries traditionally close to Iran, or in close geographic proximity, but also from Africa and South America. Alongside the increase in the number of contingents, the teaching platform was extended. The broadened recruitment is going hand in hand with an upgrading of the level of training offered – or imposed – and its diversification.

All these actions are organized and carried out in Iran, to allow supervision and to maximize the chances of success. The number of camps bears witness to the new scope of training, as there were dozens, including fourteen main camps, spread throughout the country, mainly around Tehran, plus in the north, not far from the Caspian Sea, and in the north-east, in the province of Khorasan.

According to a report recently published in Washington, the information concurs to estimate the annual recruitment of volunteers at same several hundred, who come from Iraq, the preferred source, from Syria, from the Houthi tribe in Yemen, from Afghanistan and from Lebanon, where cooperation with Hezbollah goes back thirty years. Other volunteers come from Venezuela, Uruguay and Paraguay, as well as from Bolivia, a country with a regime similar to that of Tehran. It seems that these volunteers have already carried out missions for the Iranian regime and, in their case, it is a question of ongoing training rather than initial training. Generally, the foreigners, who are not necessarily Muslim and, rarer still, Shiite, are kept in isolation, and their presence, like their identities, remains secret. The Imam Ali garrison – which will be looked at later – is the principal guerilla and terrorism training center, and is the preferred facility to host them. This base extends over ten hectares, and it also accommodates other IRGC units.

The training itself is inspired by foreign models – we know, for example, that cooperation with the Lebanese Hezbollah has been taken far – including a short basic primary course lasting less than two months, which equates to France's common basic training (FCB), followed by full military training that can last as long as a year. The initial training is given in the form of a course devoted to the promotion of fundamentalism and terrorism. It generally takes place at the Imam Ali Academy or at the Baadindeh Centre at Varamin. It also gives a lot of time to sport. The technical training is spread through several centers. It is usually focused on the use of heavy weapons, equipment such as drones, rockets and missile launchers. The latter subject involves a theoretical part carried out with a simulator, and a practical part dispensed at the Semnan military base. As it is necessary to diversify the potentials of each combat trainee, "special subjects" are taught in ad hoc centers – they include combat swimming, parachuting and VIP bodyguard training, delicately entitled *protocol*, and operations in urban environments, with specific instruction in the use of motorcycles, freeing hostages and sniping, plus survival training. This instruction looks very similar to the Soviet *Spetnatzs* training and covers adaptation to clandestinity where necessary in hostile circumstances.

Training sessions can host up to several hundred trainees, if necessary, depending on the command's assessment. The largest contingent recorded came from Syria, and numbered 230. Events in Bahrain explain the large number of volunteers from that emirate – most of them Shiite – where the uprising during the Arab spring was suppressed by the Saudi army, but where Tehran is seeking to overturn the government at any cost. In the same way, Afghan fighters sent to Syria receive infantry training, close-quarters combat and training on the use of automatic weapons and heavy weapons. The high throughput training means that from 200 to 300 men can be sent to Syria every week.

This training was entrusted for a long time to a veteran of the various wars that the regime has conducted on all fronts. His personality clarifies and illustrates the value (in every sense of the term) that the IRGC places on this essential feature. He is General Khosrow Orouj, who was for long the key partner of the Lebanese Hezbollah, and the friend of Imad Mughniyah, a specialist in booby-trapping cars who died when his own vehicle exploded. In a recent declaration, Orouj recalled his commitment to the preparation of special forces, and in particular said, "When Khamenei visited the Quds Force, the only unit he applauded was the IRGC training unit.", thereby recognizing the Leader's personal involvement in the Iranian terrorist training process.

This attitude on the part of the leading personality of the Islamic Republic – which we really ought to call *Islamist* - is inherent in the logic and the continuity of a policy of eradication of all forms of opposition and/or of adversity that Khomeini initiated and then pushed to intolerable lengths by ordering the massacre of political prisoners in July 1988. It is almost incomprehensible that the international community did not react when, at the same time, it held Iraq guilty of aggression against a petro-monarchy, and then totally ruined that developing country. The United States led this suicidal and retrograde undertaking, which only served the interests of neighboring Iran. As regards the second Gulf war, for which the justifications were based on state lies – which is what they call a *"forfeiture"*, or breach of faith, in France – the two countries, the democracy (US) and the autocracy (Iran), agreed to reduce the Iranian resistance to dust; the worst is that France believed it was a good idea to play a part in it all. What caused the demonic plot to fail was the commitment of a population in solidarity with *"its"* resistance and the mindfulness of some American military leaders. The truth is coming to light, at the cost of new atrocities by the regime and the sacrifice of hundreds of PMOI militants. Not uncourageously, President Bush recognized his error; British Prime Minister Tony Blair could only follow suit.

But the evil is done: Iran, - to call it the *evil power* is insufficient – found itself relieved of its closest potential enemies – Afghanistan to the east and Iraq to the west – without firing a shot or spending a toman. Better yet, it has been taking advantage of diplomatic apathy and the greed of the oil companies to move its pawns on the Near East chessboard and install itself durably on the Mediterranean coast and even in the Arabian Peninsula. It would like to become the dominant power in the region.

In the other corner is the US, which proclaimed itself master of the world but is failing in everything it undertakes: a balanced conclusion to the Palestinian conflict, the eradication of Islamist terrorism, a return to peace in Afghanistan, and stability of the allied Arab governments (Tunisia and Egypt). The fault lies in a diplomacy rooted in outdated positions, such as the permanence of the rivalry with Russia, the policy of containment, and the superiority complex vis-à-vis China, which is paying full attention. The carry-over effects of the conflicts into which successive presidents have thrust themselves are especially worrying because they affect the American consciousness. If there is a people which cannot live without its consciousness, it is the American people, simply because they have not yet managed fusion of their diverse components and, as in Tocqueville's century, they need to be nationalistic or even chauvinistic.

In 2009, in the favored circles of New England, there emerged a new figure. He was not a descendant of slaves, as his color would have you believe, but a black semi-African, the descendant of a recent immigrant. He was full of talent and generosity, and supported by a wife who is a pure intellectual, who peacefully accepts the fact that she is the descendant of slaves. Barack Obama had little difficulty in distancing himself from his predecessor, but he underestimated the weight of tradition in a country which seeks to create new ones. Above all, he entrusted his foreign policy to Hilary Clinton, his adversary in the Democratic Party primaries, and he broke the most-elementary rules of prudence when he followed his British and French allies into the Libyan venture, the consequences of which are still unfathomable. Furthermore he admitted it, with the frankness typical of America's political men, which is to their credit. But the most dangerous, because the most insidious, is yet to come: that's the agreement with the Iranian government on nuclear power, concluded as a bet on the good faith of the other party.

The naivety of those in government is staggering - the previous episodes of their biased confrontation with the clerical regime should have been a convincing example of its bad faith. Rarely has a country been open to abuse in such a way, and in such a short time. Barack Obama should have been able to remember the invasion of the US Embassy in Tehran, carried out by "demonstrators" who were soon to be found in commanding positions in the Iranian state, with Mahmoud Ahmadinejad at their head, the vicious game by which the mullahs encouraged Jimmy Carter's defeat in the Presidential election, Irangate, the attacks in

Lebanon carried out in the name of Iran *the clement and merciful*, the murder of the protestant pastors, the 1988 massacre, the nuclear cooperation with Dr. Abdul-Qader Khan and North Korea, the threats to Israel and the title "Great Satan" pronounced by Khomeini in person. He should have been able to call to mind so many facts, a single one of which would require the break-off of inoperable diplomatic relations. He preferred to earn a Nobel Prize for complacency by pushing his western partners to sign a deal that not all of them wanted – certainly not France, in any event. He bet on the good faith of institutional tricksters, without a careful study of the conspirational conditions in which Iran had advanced so considerably over the last thirty years.

His successor in the White House is manifestly not cast in the same mold. This false *self-made man* is a true businessman, and he did not win the most-observed election in the world without ability. First of all, he knew how to translate the disenchantment of the American middle class, dramatically penalized by the Sub-Primes Crisis, and deprived of their retirement pensions because of it. On the other hand, his ignorance of the arcane ways of American political life has made this seventy-something look like a new man. He has no great political culture; he can only oppose his good sense to the policy arguments of his democratic adversary, who is fully aware of the subtleties of foreign policy.

Donald Trump, whose name, personality and family make us laugh, has the faith of a neophyte. He imagines that it's enough to command to be obeyed. He holds the reins of the machinery of the most powerful state in the world in his hands, and he uses it as if it were a Christmas toy, without reading the instructions. However, he also has an appointment with history: the deadlines are close and formidable. Consequently, we are expecting action on a few affairs that will be significant as regards his capacity and his will - Israel, relations with Russia and the Iran nuclear issue.

He should not deal with this matter as Barak Obama did. He is suspicious of the Iranian leadership, and so is his entourage. It must be said that he belongs to the Republican family, firmer in both speech and attitude than the Democrats. Certainly, in the United States, the idea of party politics is appreciably different from ours. These huge formations have fuzzy outlines, tropisms which are at once both common and different. Geographic origin counts for at least as much as harnessing yourself to the Democratic donkeys or the Republican elephants. The south, where the smoke of the civil war still lingers in the Everglades, remains conservative, whilst New England is soundly liberal. This can mean that a democrat in Houston may be further to the right than a republican in Chicago - as far as these labels have any meaning on the other side of the Atlantic.

With this reservation, we can take it as read that the Republican Party overall will be less receptive than their Democrat opponents to the sirens from Persia, and consequently firmer regarding principles. This forecast appears to be justified, as the new President is envisioning scrapping the agreement of July 14, 2015 and, in addition, some sixty members of the House of Representatives – mostly Republican – are demanding that those responsible for the 1988 massacre be brought before the international courts of justice. This is a considerable event in itself, that would take on another dimension if the serving President of the United States could carry out his threat. Charging those of the Islamic Republic's leaders or state organizations having been responsible for criminal or terrorist actions would strengthen Donald Trump's position and boost his credibility.

These charges, which should not be considered as an ensemble but individually, are the worst to have been compiled against one country since the founding of the United Nations and the international courts. As we have seen above, proceedings can be brought for two types of offense: for criminal acts, such as the 1988 massacre and the suppression of the green revolution of 2009, and the acts of terrorism, of which the continuity has been established above.

These institutions will be judging the leaders of the IRGC, and the international courts will have to draw up the list of them. A decision will have to be taken about which court has jurisdiction: either the International Criminal Court, as established under the Treaty of Rome, which would be an unarguable choice, or else an ad hoc court, as was the case for the events in Yugoslavia and Rwanda. Unfortunately, the fact that neither the United States nor Iran ratified the Treaty of Rome has weakened that Court considerably. Here is a clear case of the selfishness which we often see, with countries contravening whatever form of international law with a clear conscience. It is absolutely shocking that we continue to judge supposed war criminals when the most-powerful states in the world are sure that they can act with impunity.

We must therefore make the best of it and be content with an accusation, even inoperable, because it will at least weaken Iran's international position. The rest is up to History.

Yves Bonnet is former governor and former Director of the Territorial Surveillance Directorate, Director of the International Center for Research and Study on Terrorism and Assistance to Victims of Terrorism.

Human rights in Iran: A review of the situation

Simin Nouri

The accession of Hassan Rouhani to the presidency of the Islamic Republic of Iran in August 2013 made some people hope for a moderate president, even dressed in clerical robes, and that he would be preferable to Mahmoud Ahmadinejad who wore a civilian suit. After eight years of the presidency of the ultra-conservative Mahmoud Ahmadinejad (2005-2013), the turbaned Rouhani was in effect immediately qualified as a "moderate" because of his stances on the nuclear issue, even though everyone knew that they were dictated by the State's number one, the "Supreme Leader" Ali Khamenei in person. But let's remember that this position was adopted under the pressure of international sanctions assorted with a promise: more tolerance and less repression within the country, with iron-fist governance by the leaders of the unrelenting theocracy and its Revolutionary Guards.

Rouhani also promised openness towards the outside world – notably the Western world – which was supposed to improve the country's disastrous economic situation. But any hope for moderation has steadily been dissipated by the terrifying figure of more than 2,600 hangings during his four-year mandate, which will end before the autumn of 2017. According to human rights organizations, Iran tops even China, the country with the biggest population in the world, for the number of executions per capita.

Having held key jobs for long years in the military and security institutions of the Iranian regime, Hassan Rouhani is neither unknown nor a novice. The man has his roots within the establishment. He is one of the veterans of the Khomeinist theocracy that has been in power for 38 years.

The central problem in the Iran of the mullahs is, and has always been, the fact that the clerical dictatorship in power in the country brings about the predominance of *"Sharia"* in political, public and private life. Literally translated as "the path to respecting divine law", Sharia covers all standards and rules – doctrinal as well as social, cultural and relational. Any non-submission of the people – *Umma* – to these rules is subject to punishments of incommensurable severity.

Knowing the extremely-limited role of the President in a State governed by the doctrine of *Velayat-e faqih* – the absolute ascendancy of a religious Supreme Leader – the old-timer Rouhani is perfectly aware that he can neither touch the legislation in force, based on "divine laws", nor undertake any reform that might affect the political, social, legal, cultural and other fundamental principles and laws.

Moreover, when one looks back at the last four years of the present Iranian President, one has to acknowledge that – despite his electoral promises – his term in office has not "softened" the repressive legislation in application or lightened the concrete mantle that weighs on freedoms in the Iranian society. He has instead fulfilled one precise mission: that of resolving "with all moderation" the dilemma of the Iranian nuclear program with the American "Great Satan", with the aim of getting the international sanctions lifted.

Velayat-e faqih in conflict with the universal acceptance of fundamental rights

In profound contradiction with the universal principles of the rights of the human, the articles of law written into the Constitution and the Penal and Civil Codes of *Velayat-e faqih* – the absolute authority of the religious guide from the clergy – preach a theocratic vision based on the laws of *Sharia*, the brutal repression of opponents and resistors, corporal punishment, and the absence of individual and public liberties. This entire "legal system", with its discriminations based on religion, political opinion and – above all – gender, has been instituted in the name of "divine commandments".

A – Non-respect for the right to Life

According to the view of the Khomeinist clergy, the lives of citizens who commit "grave sins" or who oppose this inhumane system are worth nothing. Death sentences are often pronounced based on an accusation of "war against God" (*moharebeh*) or "corruption on earth" (*mofsedfelarz*) – ambiguous terms with no detailed legal definition, harking from another age.

It is important to note that certain concepts of "sin", according to the "religious" view of things, have been officially instituted in the legislation of the Islamic Republic as crimes and offences of legal nature, punishable by penalties ranging from lashes with a whip to death, not to mention heavy prison sentences after the accused's appearance before a court.

Thus, people can be arrested for having drunk alcoholic beverages, or for having committed "adultery", or for having smoked or eaten in public during the month of Ramadan. The same applies for people accused of apostasy or homosexual acts.

In the case of people having drunk alcohol, "adultery" between unmarried persons, or non-compliance in public with fasting during Ramadan, people found "guilty" are condemned to beatings involving hundreds of lashes, or even more. A person who is arrested a third time for having drunk alcohol will simply be condemned to death!

In cases of "adultery" between married persons, death by stoning is pronounced. All death sentences are supposed to be confirmed by the Supreme Court, chaired by a mullah of high rank. The argument advanced by certain representatives of the legal power or executive of the Khomeinist regime to the international authorities, on stoning, advances the idea that only isolated cases in the most-backward parts of the country are involved. But these arguments don't stand up to examination. This is indeed a case of legislation in force within the scope of the "Law of Islamic Punishments", having been voted for by the Islamic Republic's parliament.

The Death Penalty

The death sentence continues to be applied by hanging within prisons and, sometimes, in public. A death sentence is pronounced by the judiciary after hearings that are generally unfair and, very often, without the presence of a lawyer for the defendant. The judges of so-called Revolutionary Courts are nearly all from the clergy, and have a particularly free hand when it comes to accusation, the preparation of the case, and the sentencing. The verdict is often pronounced on the basis of the accused's own "confessions" obtained after having spent many months or even years in imprisonment, in extremely harsh conditions and without having had advice from a defense lawyer. Most of the time, the accused suffers barbaric tortures – notably in the case of political prisoners and prisoners of conscience.

According to human rights organizations, at least 543 prisoners were executed during 2016 in Iran[89]. Among the victims were ten women and at least five individuals whose alleged crimes were committed when they were minors.

Over 138 executions were recorded during the first two months of 2017[90].

Just before International Women's Day, the authorities hanged two female prisoners in the north of Iran, on March 5, 2017.

- **Execution of minors**

The age of criminal responsibility is set at 15 lunar years for boys and 9 lunar years for girls. Over the course of the last decade, the Iranian authorities have executed the largest number of juvenile delinquents in the world. Despite an absolute ban on this practice in international law, the Penal Code of the Islamic Republic continues to explicitly maintain capital punishment for minors.

According to Amnesty International, during the year 2016 at least five minors are believed to have been executed in Iran [Ali-Reza Madadpour, Hassan Afshar, Houshang Zare, Mehdi Rajaie, Khaled Kordi,...], and at least 78 people are thought to have been condemned to death for crimes committed when they were less than 18 years of age, although the true figure could be much higher. [91]

---

[89] Iran 2016/2017 annual report, Amnesty international
https://www.amnesty.org/en/countries/middle-east-and-north-africa/iran/report-iran/

[90] AFIF INFOS monthly newsletter, January and February 2017, femmesiraniennes.blogspot.fr

[91] Growing up on death row: The death penalty and juvenile offenders in Iran, Amnesty International, January 26, 2016, index number: MDE 13/3112/2016

Some of these young people stay on death row for years, while others are hanged when they reach the age of 18.

In its final findings published in January 2017, the UN Committee on the Rights of the Child (CRC) expressed great anxiety about the subject of the continued execution of minors, and requested the Iranian Government to withdraw its reservations concerning non-compliance with the Committee's measures. It also exhorted the Iranian Government to raise the age of criminal responsibility, with no discrimination between boys and girls.

In a statement published January 17, 2017, the Office of the United Nations High Commissioner for Human Rights (OHCHR) and a committee of experts demanded that the Iranian authorities put an end to the execution of minors.[92]

On February 2, 2017, the UN experts on human rights exhorted Iran to permanently halt the imminent execution of the delinquent minor, Hamid Ahmadi.[93]

- **Collective and public executions**

Most victims are condemned to death for drug-related offenses although, according to international law on human rights, these offenses are not considered to be "the most serious crimes".

On September 11, 2016, 17 prisoners were hanged at the same time at the Vakil-Abad prison in Mashhad. Eleven young people were executed collectively on May 25, 2016, in Gohardasht prison. When the entire globe was celebrating International Human Rights Day on December 10, the *Velayat-e faqih* regime collectively executed 11 other prisoners at Gohardasht.[94]

---

[92] Press statement from the Office of the United Nations High Commissioner for Human Rights, January 17, 2017

[93] Report of the OHCHR, Geneva, February 2, 2017

[94] Iran Human Rights Annual Report /2016

Notwithstanding the colossal financial and technical aid that the Iranian State has been receiving for many years from the United Nations Office on Drugs and Crime (UNODC), the European Union and various other countries, for combating drug trafficking and stemming the flow of drugs crossing its border with Afghanistan, the number of hangings has not ceased rising over the last few years.

In this country in which an "offending" web user is quickly located by the agents of the Intelligence Ministry, the big narcotics traffickers are conveniently continuing their macabre business while minor dealers possessing just a few grams of drugs are executed.

- **Execution for murder and** *moharebeh*

In homicide cases, it is the principle of the law of retribution – *Qesas* – that is applied, unless the family of the victim pardons the murderer or accepts compensation – *diyeh* or "blood money".

Thus, by applying the law of retribution, the criminal legislation and the judiciary of the Khomeinist state reduces the justice of the general interest – intended to protect society against crime and delinquency, and to reform offenders – to a simple question of personal vengeance. This is why one can often see a murderer freed if his friends or family offer the sum (blood money) demanded by the family or friends of the victim. In other cases, the murderer is hanged in the presence of the victim's family and friends, who sometimes ask to be allowed to themselves place the noose around the condemned person's neck.

This is therefore individual justice derived from a medieval conception.

The extremely vague concept of *moharebeh* (war against God), "propaganda against the authorities", "plotting" or "intelligence-sharing" with foreign powers – which, in some cases, simply means the fact of having granted interviews to western media – or else the concept of "insults to Islam" or "blasphemy" are also among the accusations for which capital punishment is possible.

Among the 25 Sunni prisoners executed collectively on August 2, 2016, at Gohardasht prison (to the west of Tehran), two were hanged for "outrages" against the Prophet of Islam. The United Nations High Commissioner for Human Rights, Zeid Ra'ad Al Hussein, condemned these hangings and, on August 5, 2016, said: "The application of overly broad and vague criminal charges, coupled with a disdain for the rights of the accused to due process and a fair trial have in these cases led to a grave injustice".

- **Execution for adultery and homosexuality**

Article 102 of the Islamic Penal Code states that, "Stoning until death ensues is the punishment reserved for adultery. The male and the female adulterers are to be buried in a hole filled with sand, the former up to the waist and the latter to below the breasts, and are thereafter to be stoned".

Because polygamy is legal in Iran, men can easily avoid death by stoning. Polygamy places men and women on an unequal footing for the same crime. A married man who commits adultery can produce a certificate of new marriage and thereby escape the penalty, whereas a married woman adulterer would be stoned to death. Several women have suffered this inhuman act before a slow and painful death.

Since 2015, at least two women accused of adultery have been condemned to stoning. In its "response" to the Special Rapporteur, the Iranian Government states that "condemnation for acts of adultery is in conformity with its interpretation of Islamic law, and that stoning constitutes an effective means of dissuasion".

At this time, at least one Iranian woman – Fariba Khaleghi – remains condemned to death by stoning.[95]

Torture and cruel, inhuman or degrading treatments

Amputations, eye-gouging and beatings are punishments from the Middle Ages and are provided for by the legislation of the Supreme Leader's regime.

The official Iranian media have reported two eye-gougings in November 2016. They also reported two amputations of fingers in December, inflicted on two prisoners held in Oroumieh prison, in the presence of seventy other prisoners, who were forced to watch the torture.

Several other condemnations to beating during the course of 2016 were reported by rights organizations and local media.

- **Denial of access to medical care; a means of pressure or physical torture**

Physical and mental torture or bad treatment with the purpose of forcing confessions during detention in custody are frequent, as is extension of the period of detainees' custody and the withholding of appropriate and necessary medical care from them.

In the conclusion of an investigation published on July 18, 2016, Amnesty International explains that "Cumulatively, these practices and conditions mean that political prisoners in Iran are put at risk of needless death, permanent disability or other irreparable damage to their health." [96]

---

[95] Report of the UN Secretary General, September 6, 2016

[96] *Health taken hostage: Cruel denial of medical care in Iran's prisons*, Report by Amnesty International, July 18, 2016

The international community thus confirms the clandestine and sporadic reports coming out of Iran from political prisoners and their family and friends, about the inhuman treatment meted out by the prison authorities, which deliberately deprive prisoners of medical care. The premeditated nature of their practically-systematic refusals is another form of putting detainees to death.

- The young Kurdish activist, Ms Zeinab Jalalian, who was tortured for having admitted to being a member of a Kurdish opposition group, has been deprived of medical care for a long time. She is at the point of losing her sight in prison.

- To obtain the possibility of contact with her two children, the human rights activist, Ms Narges Mohammadi, went on hunger strike for 20 days in June 2016. She is a prisoner of conscience having been sentenced to one year of prison for "propaganda against the authorities", five years imprisonment for "meeting and collusion against national security", and ten years for the founding and running of an illegal group. According to Article 134 of the Islamic Penal Code, sentences are executed simultaneously; consequently; Mrs Mohammadi has to serve ten more years in jail.

- Ms Maryam Akbari-Monfared is a political prisoner serving a sentence of 15 years of incarceration, accused of membership in a banned opposition group, the People's Mojahedin Organization of Iran (PMOI); she was deprived of treatment after having published an open letter demanding justice and the truth about the fate of her brothers and sisters, who were executed in 1988.

- Mrs Nazanin Ratcliffe, an Iranian-British human rights activist whose detention was judged arbitrary by the United Nations Working Group on Arbitrary Detention, was obliged to choose between being separated from her daughter during her time in prison, or signing a document renouncing all her rights with regard to her child.

B – Non-respect for the right to equality

Discrimination based on gender is institutionalized by the Khomeinist regime. The profoundly-misogynistic laws have set back the gains from over one hundred years of campaigning by women in Iran's history.

The principal legal source of the central misogynistic conception is to be found in the Constitution, the fundamental law of the *Velayat-e-faqih* system. It forbids women the right of holding the Presidency of the Republic and becoming a magistrate.

This contravenes Article 20 of the said Constitution, which stipulates that "All members of the nation, women or men, are equal and under the protection of the Law. They all have human, political, economic, social and cultural rights, <u>in keeping with Islamic criteria</u>".

The proclamation of rights is thus a simple declaration in the Constitution. It is devoid of sense in practice, notably because of the words "in keeping with Islamic criteria" – in other words, subject to the goodwill of the clergy responsible for the interpretation of *Sharia*. It brings no improvement to the status of Iranian women, who have always been considered to be second-class citizens since the advent of the Islamic Republic.

Other discriminatory laws in the Civil and Penal Codes highlight the strongly-misogynous character of the State:

Civil Code

Article 907 – A woman inherits half of what a man does;

- A husband can forbid his spouse from practicing any profession or occupation that goes against the family's interests or detracts from the spouse's dignity;

Paragraph – A woman cannot travel without her husband's permission;

- A man can refuse to financially support a spouse who is not fulfilling her conjugal duties;

Article 1060 – A Muslim woman does not have the right to marry a non-Muslim;

Paragraph – Polygamy is permitted by law for men, who can legally have up to four wives;

Article 1075 – Temporary marriage [*sigheh*] is legal for a period of time ranging from one hour to ninety-nine years;

- A man can contract as many temporary marriages as he wants. He can end the contract when he wants. A woman cannot;

Article 1133 – A man can divorce [repudiate] his wife at any time, with no prior or legal condition;

- A wife must be able to provide valid arguments for requesting divorce;

Penal Code

Article 237 – The testimony of a man is worth that of two women, even in the case of premeditated murder;

Article 638 – It is obligatory for women to wear the veil in public;

"Improperly-veiled women arrested in the act in public are subject to a penalty of imprisonment ranging from ten days to two months and 74 lashes of a whip. The payment of fines from 5,000 to 50,000 tomans enables the punishments to be escaped."

Although it is a member of the UN Commission on the Status of Women (CSW), Iran still has not ratified the Convention on the Elimination of All Forms of Discrimination Against Women (CEDAW).

According to official sources within the Iranian government, 60% of women in Iran are victims of domestic violence, early marriages are frequent, and 21% of Iranian girls aged less than 19 are married.

Some 40% of women with qualifications from higher education are unemployed. The percentage of working women aged from 15 to 64 in the employment market does not exceed 17%.

The representation of women in public life is only 6%.

Iran has one of the highest rates of suicide among women in the world.

Discrimination based on religion

The situation of religious minorities, whether recognized or not recognized, remains a serious concern.

Followers of the Baha'i faith continue to suffer systematic discrimination. The Baha'i faith, with 350,000 members, is not recognized by the Constitution of the Islamic Republic of Iran.

Considered by the clergy to be "infidels" or members of a "deviant sect", Baha'i citizens are accused of apostasy, among other things. They are harassed and deprived of legal protection.

Nearly 90 Baha'i people – including seven community leaders – are currently in prison. They are being held for accusations such as "spying", "breaching national security", "spreading anti-government propaganda", etc. These charges are in fact due purely to their religious beliefs and practices.

In addition to arbitrary arrests, detentions and other actions, the Iranian authorities often destroy Baha'i cemeteries and religious sites, and carry out operations that have major consequences for their community and employment rights.

In November 2016, the authorities indefinitely closed dozens of companies belonging to Baha'i people and put pressure on other business owners to dismiss their Baha'i employees.

Baha'i students are very frequently expelled from universities and other further education establishments. To be able to continue their studies, they have to renounce their faith in writing.

Nearly eight million **Sunni Iranians**, are treated as second-class citizens, even though they are Muslim. No Sunni candidates can stand for presidential election, and no Sunni has been a member of the government since the advent of the Islamic Republic.

Although many of them live in big Iranian cities, they do not have the right to have their own places of worship in Tehran, Mashhad, Isfahan and Shiraz.

The severe treatments meted out to **Christian converts** of Islamic origin, and to the members of various "Sufi" groups, by the authorities and members of the clergy are also worrying. Christian converts are prosecuted for apostasy. It is obvious that accusation of apostasy – for which the penalty is death – is a clear and brutal violation of the right to freedom of religion or belief.

Followers of **Sufism** (a peace-advocating form of Islamic mysticism) continue to suffer harassment, arrests and arbitrary detentions, and are often accused of "propaganda against the State" and "actions against national security".

Discrimination based on ethnic origin

"Violations of the rights of ethnic minorities continue to be reported in the country. Nearly one fifth of executions having taken place in Iran in 2016 involved Kurdish prisoners. Out of these executions, 21 involved the crime of "*moharebeh*" and membership to a Kurdish political party. Kurdish political prisoners account for nearly half of the total number of political prisoners in Iran."[97]

In 2016, the Iranian security forces killed 51 *koulbar* and wounded 71 others, which is about twice as many as the preceding year. The *koulbaran* of Kurdistan – Kurdish itinerant peddlers who engage in goods trafficking across the border – are also the targets of ethnic discrimination. Because of the high unemployment rate in the towns and cities of Iranian Kurdistan, this activity is generally the only way they have to meet their needs and those of their family.

C - Non-respect for the right to freedom

- **Freedom of opinion**

Legislation strictly bans political parties, except those having fulfilled draconian conditions. All applicants are required to explicitly state their upholding of the Constitution and the principle of *Velayat-e faqih* in their statutes, manifestos, charters and founding documents.

They have to obtain two permits from a committee of five members drawn from members of the Parliament, the judiciary and the Ministry of the Interior.

The Law also obliges applicants to provide information about their points of view and positions on cultural, economic, social, political, administrative and legal issues in the country.

Article 5 of the law lists the categories of individuals who are banned from belonging to political parties, which includes individuals suspected by the security forces and the Ministry of Intelligence of being "spies" or "agents" of foreign nations.

---

[97] Report of the Special Rapporteur on the situation of human rights in the Islamic Republic of Iran, Human Rights Council Thirty-fourth session, February 27 to March 24, 2017, and March 6, 2017

- **Freedom of expression**

According to the 2016 report from Reporters Without Borders (RSF) about the world classification for press freedom, RSF places Iran in 169th position out of a total of 180.[98]

The report says that despite an improvement in its international relations, Iran is still one of the most-repressive countries in the world concerning freedom of information. News publications and journalists are still victims of the war between the various clans at the heights of power. The 1986 press law, (amended in 2000 and 2009 to include online publications) allows the authorities to ensure that news providers do not "attack the Islamic Republic," "insult the Supreme Leader" or "disseminate false information."

The last six months of 2016 were marked by a new series of arrests and detentions of writers, journalists, activists on social media, and defenders of human rights.

In August 2016, the Court of Appeal of the city of Saveh confirmed the sentence of a beating with 459 lashes of a whip upon the journalist and blogger Mohammad-Reza Fathi for having criticized members of the municipal council.[99]

Under the terms of Articles 609 and 698 of the Islamic Penal Code, the criticism of senior public officials and the publication of false information are punishable by 74 lashes.

According to Iranian media and Reporters Without Borders, at least 24 journalists, bloggers and social media activists were arrested, held or condemned in December 2016, and many others

---

[98] Classement mondial de la liberté de la presse 2016, Rapport RSF

[99] *Press freedom violations recounted in real time January 2016*, RSF, August 22, 2016

are being regularly subjected to harassment, intimidation, surveillance or even interrogation.

Hassan Rouhani's government is continuing to restrict access to information, by filtering websites and throttling Internet access bandwidth. Some 5 million websites – of which 500 cover social issues, the arts and popular culture – are being blocked by the government.

Two human rights activists who are married together, Mr. Arash Sadeghi and Mrs. Golrokh Ebrahimi Iraee, were imprisoned in June and October 2016. Mr. Sadeghi is believed to have been tortured during the interrogations, and Mrs. Ebrahimi was held secretly in isolation for 20 days. Both were denied access to a lawyer during the interrogations and when they appeared before the Revolutionary Court in Tehran.

Mr. Sadeghi was sentenced to 15 years of incarceration at Evin prison for accusations such as "propaganda against the system", "organization, assembly and collusion against national security", and "insulting the founder of the Islamic Republic". He was condemned for having sent emails and posted Facebook messages to human rights activists abroad.

His wife was sentenced to five years of prison for having written a fictional work on stoning in Iran. [100]

The Iranian media have reported that *hojatoleslam* Ahmad Montazeri, son of Ayatollah Hossein-Ali Montazeri – one of the founders of the Islamic Republic – was condemned on November 27, 2016, by the Special Clerical Court of Qom, to 21 years imprisonment for "endangering national security" and "leaking secrets of the Islamic state".[101]

---

[100] Center for Human Rights in Iran, January 10, 2017

[101] Iranian Students' News Agency (ISNA), November 27, 2016

He had published an audio recording on August 2, 2016, in which his father denounced the mass execution of political prisoners in the summer of 1988.

In this recording, one can hear Hossein-Ali Montazeri qualify this massacre as "the greatest crime committed under the Islamic Republic". He states, with anger, to his interlocutors, who are members of a 'death committee' appointed by Khomeini to apply the *fatwa*: "In my opinion, the greatest crime committed under the Islamic Republic, from the beginning of the Revolution until now, is this crime committed by you .... In my opinion, the greatest crime committed during the Islamic Republic, for which history will condemn us, has been committed by you. Your (names) will in the future be etched in the annals of history as criminals."

In this recording of conversations lasting some forty minutes, Montazeri denounces the cruelty of the regime, demanding the persons responsible: "Why did you execute someone you had been sentenced to ten years of prison?" He warns them that the fact of forbidding family visits for two months will avail them nothing, and that these families will hold them accountable. He notably mentions the execution of girls as young as 15 and pregnant women.

This revelation broke a taboo and raised an uproar in Iranian society, in which the mention of this tragedy of Iran's modern history was in the realm of the forbidden.

Ahmad Montazeri finally had to be released, albeit temporarily, upon the Supreme Leader's permission – officially for having undertaken the commitment not to act against the Islamic Republic, whereas Mr. Montazeri claims he has not undertaken any commitment. The regime does not feel able to allow further disturbance of a page of history that could cost it dearly, especially as the main parties responsible for the massacre – such as the incumbent Minister of Justice Mostafa Pourmohammadi – hold key positions in the existing power structure.

The families and close associates of more than 30,000 political prisoners executed over the space of a few months in 1988 decry the regime's impunity in having carried out this unprecedented massacre, and are demanding an international inquiry so that the people who ordered it and who carried it out can be brought to justice, some of who still occupy senior positions in government – notably the Minister of Justice of the current administration.

In a report published March 8, 2017, entitled "Iran: Repression of Those Seeking Truth and Justice for 1980s Killings Needs to Stop", Amnesty International states:

"In this joint statement, 20 human rights groups call on the Iranian authorities to stop the harassment, intimidation and prosecution of human rights defenders seeking truth and justice on behalf of individuals who were summarily executed or forcibly disappeared during the 1980s and their families. Over the past few months, several human rights defenders have been subjected to harassment, reprisals or prosecution on vague national security-related charges for their peaceful efforts to learn the fate and whereabouts of their loved ones."[102]

The eminent lawyer of Pakistani origin, Mrs. Asma Jahangir – the new UN Special Rapporteur on the human rights situation in Iran – has drawn the world's attention to this issue and informed the UN Human Rights Council session in Geneva about the "execution of thousands of political dissidents in 1988, who had already been tried and sentenced to prison in detention facilities throughout the country."

It was precisely in Geneva that an NGO, Justice for the Victims of the 1988 Massacre in Iran (JVMI), presented a report in which it claims a crime against humanity has been committed and calls on

---

[102] Amnesty International report of March 8, 2017, index number: MDE 13/5840/2017

https://www.amnesty.org/en/documents/mde13/5840/2017/en/

the High Commissioner for Human Rights to put an end to the impunity of the parties responsible by commissioning an independent inquiry.

Conclusion

Reviewing human rights in a nation such as Iran requires an examination of the effect of the laws in force, and of the existing legal and political context, as well as a clear knowledge of the practices towards citizens in connection with human rights, with reference to rules of international law and to recommendations published by the international institutions safeguarding human rights.

In the particular case of the Islamic Republic of Iran, which has now existed for 38 years, since a popular revolt against the monarchical dictatorship during which the population was demanding freedom and independence, we have an anachronistic governmental entity of which the founding principle of *Velayat-e faqih* and the Constitution go against most internationally-recognized norms. One can speak of standards such as the Universal Declaration of Human Rights, values constituting modern civilization, and international rules and conventions intended to facilitate relations between nations under the auspices of democracy, human rights and respect for individuals, including their right to life and to physical and mental integrity, peace, normal diplomatic relations, etc.

The Islamic Republic of Iran has been condemned 63 times by UN institutions, for flagrant human rights violations. The most recent condemnation was the resolution adopted on December 17, 2016, by the United Nations General Assembly.

In view of the Iranian Government's violations of its citizens' fundamental rights – which has become systematic – the UN has long maintained the appointment of a Special Rapporteur to observe and verify the application of rules governing human rights in the Islamic Republic of Iran.

While the Iranian Government is granting tourist visas more easily, to present an appropriate – albeit misleading – image to international opinion, visa applications by these Special Rapporteurs have all been rejected to date, to prevent them seeing the reality on the ground. Exactly the same applies to visa applications by Special Rapporteurs monitoring: the independence of judges and lawyers; the extrajudicial, summary or arbitrary executions; freedom of religion or belief; minority issues; and promotion and protection of the right to freedom of opinion and expression.

The so-called "pragmatic" government of Hassan Rouhani also refused to grant an entry visa to working groups on the issue of discrimination against women in law and in practice, on Enforced or Involuntary Disappearances, and on Arbitrary Detention so that these groups could visit Iran to investigate and observe in the field.

In her report published on March 6, 2017, Ms Asma Jahangir, the UN Special Rapporteur on the human rights situation in Iran, said that since her recent appointment (in September 2016), she has been contacted by a large number of Iranians living both abroad and inside Iran. She says that she is disturbed by the level of fear of those who try to communicate with her, and that interlocutors living outside and inside the country expressed fear of reprisals against them or their family members living inside the country.

The deeply-concerning statements by Ms Jahangir reveal the climate of terror among Iranians, even those in exile. The figures and the statistics about the victims of the constantly-deteriorating human rights situation in Iran are only the tip of the iceberg. They are testimonies and revelations from people daring to take the risk of providing information. Human rights activists often point out that the real figures for these violations are much higher.

Looking beyond the numbers, there is the suffering – the immense human suffering perceptible behind the thousands of victims, detainees, beatings, disappearances, etc., and the scars that mark and continue to mark Iranian society.

The Special Rapporteur "regrets that the information she received did not reveal any notable improvement in the situation of human rights in the country". She also notes that "The situation relating to independence of judges and lawyers, freedom of expression and use of arbitrary detention continues to be a matter of serious concern. She notes that some measures are under way, but their implementation and effectiveness is yet to be assessed."[103]

The false distinction between "hardliners" and "moderates"

Let it be noted that, for 38 years, this "republic" with a Khomeinist ideology – which is, in reality, a theocracy – has always shown the Western world two faces. The perception of a supposedly "moderate" or "reformist" faction confronting a hardline or ultra-conservative faction would be a wrong analysis that deliberately or erroneously ignores the nature of what Khomeini has created overall. This is because the so-called "moderate" or even "pragmatic" factions are also necessarily subject to the "divine" laws that the clergy is in charge of interpreting, under <u>the absolute authority of the religious Supreme</u> Leader, regardless of what faction is favored by the result of the "popular vote".

So it should be remembered that the representatives of the purportedly "moderate" factions have on many occasions declared or claimed that laws intended to reform certain aspects of the

---

[103] Report of the Special Rapporteur on the situation of human rights in the Islamic Republic of Iran, Human Rights Council Thirty-fourth session, March 6, 2017

system were being debated or close to adoption – a maneuver that has no other purpose than preventing the voting of resolutions of condemnation by the international authorities – notably the Human Rights Council.

The mindset of certain circles in the West that have tried to divide the religious dictatorship into "goodies" and "baddies" has proven wrong. To continue to survive in the face of the modern world and the resistance of its people, this fundamentalist regime needs both its head as well as its legs. It is indivisible.

The failure of the policy of complacency

In the face of the dark realization that this clerical regime is one of the leading violators of human rights in the world, the reaction of the democratic and Western countries has been of a hitherto unseen feebleness. Diplomats from these countries have preferred to initially open "critical" dialogue, subsequently followed by "constructive" dialogue with the mullahs, in the hope of achieving an improvement in their behavior, both within and outside the country, while continuing to advance their nations' economic and trade agendas. In short, there has been a policy of complacency that has always been interpreted as a sign of weakness of its interlocutors by the religious dictatorship existing in Iran.

The human rights situation in Iran has long been placed on the back burner by successive governments in the free world. This was notably the case when one President, Mullah Mohammad Khatami, came to power (1997-2005), and when the incumbent "moderate/pragmatic" President Rouhani entered office. This issue has been particularly eclipsed by the negotiations on the regime's nuclear program, and because of its destabilizing role in the Middle East region and beyond. The holders of power in Iran have managed not only to take 80 million Iranians hostage, but also to place bonds on the Western democracies.

Since the agreement on the Iranian nuclear program on July 14, 2015, the prospect of a gallop by a Western economy parched for growth towards the thronging market in Iran has faded from view. The deal was qualified as a triumph by the "reformers" camp over the "conservative" camp, without pushing the thinking further and admitting that without any green light from the Supreme Leader Ali Khamenei – who had previously opened negotiations with the United States at the time of Ahmadinejad – the Rouhani administration would never have dared to sign it.

After the nuclear deal, activists and advocates agitating for rights for Iranians were invited to tone down the reports of hangings, acts of torture, withholdings of care from political prisoners and other violations, and await a hypothetical "opening-up" and future improvements in human rights by virtue of the coming and going of certain noteworthy political personalities and businessmen, and the traffic of Western tourists.

It is rather difficult to imagine how the respect that these individuals of whatever background show for the oppressors of the Iranian people would encourage the latter to change anything whatsoever in their behavior. In particular, the numerous Western political women – some of whom claim to be feminists – who wear the veil in the presence of the mullahs hotly offends the women and girls of Iran, who ceaselessly take risks by daily combating the obligatory wearing of the veil and the dress code imposed by a highly-misogynous theocracy.

After nearly two years of development of economic relations between Iran and the West, one is obliged to recognize that there has been no improvement in the living conditions of Iranian people – on the contrary, there has been a continual deterioration in rights to life, equality and freedom in Iran.

The violation of fundamental human rights and ambivalence for the Universal Declaration of Human Rights are integral to the nature and ideology of the Supreme Leader's regime and remain anchored in the fundamental precepts.

Consequently, any hope of reform to change the current situation is an illusion. Those who have believed or continue to believe in a process of moderation or opening-up are clinging to mirages that feed the condescension of Iranian leaders. The truth is actually simple. As long as this dictatorship remains in power, there will be no change in the essential domains of life of a great nation, and its aspirations for a better material and spiritual life will remain distant dreams.

None of the recommendations of international bodies and none of the appeals to successive Iranian governments on abolishing the execution of minors, establishing a moratorium on the death penalty, banning stoning and public executions, and putting an end to discrimination have been effectively followed through.

In its 'WORLD REPORT 2017' published January 12, 2017, Human Rights Watch (HRW) unequivocally states that "Despite three years in his office, President Hassan Rouhani has not delivered on his campaign promise of greater respect for civil and political rights. Executions, especially for drug-related offenses, continued at a high rate. As Rouhani faces elections for a second term in May 2017, the hardline factions that dominate the security apparatus and judiciary continued to crackdown on citizens for the legitimate exercise of their rights, in blatant disregard of international and domestic legal standards. Iranian dual nationals and citizens returning from abroad were at particular risk of arrest by intelligence authorities, accused of being "Western agents." [104]

On October 25, 2016, the European Parliament adopted the report on EU strategy towards Iran subsequent to the nuclear deal, in which it expressed its concerns about the alarming number of

---

[104] *Iran – Events of 2016*, Human Rights Watch, World Report 2017
https://www.hrw.org/world-report/2017/country-chapters/iran

executions in Iran, and called for the release of all political prisoners.[105]

The question of the worsening of human rights violations in Iran has now become a strategic issue with geopolitical consequences, not just consequences in the spheres of morality, law and modern civilization. It threatens peace and stability around the world – notably in Europe. People who are suffering daily, terrible repression and seeing their material living conditions worsen day after day could rise up against the government under the slightest impulsion. In the case of a country like Iran, which is of crucial strategic importance in the Middle East region and elsewhere in the world – as could be seen with the 1979 revolution taken over by the mullahs, and as has been seen with the revolt of the Syrian people – such a social explosion could have serious consequences for the future of dozens of nations, in both the East and the West.

Therefore, there is an immense and urgent need to make unconditional and full respect for the rights of the Iranian people a condition for any negotiations and trade agreement between the Iranian clerical dictatorship and the democratic Europe.

Simin Nouri is a member of the French Committee in Defense of Human Rights in Iran (Comité de soutien aux droits de l'homme en Iran - CSDHI). She is President of the Iranian Women's Association in France.

---

[105] Report on EU strategy vis-a-vis Iran after the nuclear agreement; http://www.europarl.europa.eu/sides/getDoc.do?pubRef, October 12, 2016